I0434938

USDA

United States
Department of
Agriculture

Forest Service

Pacific Northwest
Research Station

General Technical
Report
PNW-GTR-838

August 2011

Social Vulnerability and Climate Change: Synthesis of Literature

Kathy Lynn, Katharine MacKendrick, and Ellen M. Donoghue

Authors

Kathy Lynn is a researcher, University of Oregon Environment Studies Program and Institute for a Sustainable Environment, Eugene, OR 97403 (kathy@uoregon.edu); **Katharine MacKendrick** was a research assistant, U.S. Department of Agriculture, Forest Service, Pacific Northwest Research Station, Forestry Sciences Laboratory, P.O. Box 3890, Portland, OR 97208 and University of Oregon, Department of Planning, Public Policy and Management, Eugene, OR 97405 (katie.mackendrick@ gmail.com); and **Ellen M. Donoghue** is a research social scientist, U.S. Department of Agriculture, Forest Service, Pacific Northwest Research Station, Forestry Sciences Laboratory, P.O. Box 3890, Portland, OR 97208 (edonoghue@fs.fed.us).

Additional contributions made to this project by Kevin Belanger, graduate student, University of Oregon, Environmental Studies and Planning, Public Policy and Management Departments.

Cover photograph courtesy of Swinomish Tribal Archive.

Abstract

Lynn, Kathy; MacKendrick, Katharine; and Donoghue, Ellen M. 2011.
Social vulnerability and climate change: synthesis of literature. Gen. Tech. Rep. PNW-GTR-838. Portland, OR: U.S. Department of Agriculture, Forest Service, Pacific Northwest Research Station. 70 p.

The effects of climate change are expected to be more severe for some segments of society than others because of geographic location, the degree of association with climate-sensitive environments, and unique cultural, economic, or political characteristics of particular landscapes and human populations. Social vulnerability and equity in the context of climate change are important because some populations may have less capacity to prepare for, respond to, and recover from climate-related hazards and effects. Such populations may be disproportionately affected by climate change. This synthesis of literature illustrates information about the socioeconomic, political, health, and cultural effects of climate change on socially vulnerable populations in the United States, with some additional examples in Canada. Through this synthesis, social vulnerability, equity, and climate justice are defined and described, and key issues, themes, and considerations that pertain to the effects of climate change on socially vulnerable populations are identified. The synthesis reviews what available science says about social vulnerability and climate change, and documents the emergence of issues not currently addressed in academic literature. In so doing, the synthesis identifies knowledge gaps and questions for future research.

Keywords: Climate change, social vulnerability, Native American Indians, rural communities, urban communities.

Contents

Introduction

The effects of climate change are expected to be more severe for some segments of society than others because of geographic location, the degree of association with climate-sensitive environments, and unique cultural, economic, or political characteristics of particular landscapes and human populations. Social vulnerability and equity in the context of climate change are important because some populations may have less capacity to prepare for, respond to, and recover from climate-related hazards and effects. Such populations may be disproportionately affected by climate change.

This synthesis of literature illustrates information about the socioeconomic, political, health, and cultural effects of climate change on socially vulnerable populations in the United States, with some additional examples in Canada. Through this synthesis, social vulnerability, equity, and climate justice are defined and described, and key issues, themes, and considerations that pertain to the effects of climate change on socially vulnerable populations are identified. Based on an examination of diverse sources of information, the synthesis reviews what available science says about social vulnerability and climate change, and documents the emergence of issues not currently addressed in academic literature. In so doing, the synthesis identifies knowledge gaps and questions for future research.

Climate change has the potential to inundate, degrade, and alter the chemistry and composition of the Earth, and, in turn, affect cultures, economies, and social systems (IPCC 2007). These potential effects raise questions about how vulnerable populations will be affected, but it is unclear to what extent these questions are being acknowledged and addressed within the climate change laws and policies. Internationally, developed and developing nations are in negotiations to create a post-Kyoto climate agreement. Nationally, countries are drafting and implementing their own climate policies and plans. Locally, communities are responding to the effects of climate change that are already occurring and preparing for those projected for the future. At each level, the needs, knowledge, and voices of vulnerable populations, including indigenous peoples and resource-based communities, deserve consideration and incorporation so that climate change policy (1) ensures that all people are supported and able to act, (2) provides as robust a strategy as possible to address a rapidly changing environment, and (3) enhances equity and justice.

Purpose of the Literature Synthesis

The purpose of this document is to contribute to the debate, dialogue, and efforts associated with climate change policy and program development by providing a synthesis of key literature related to the social vulnerability of indigenous peoples and urban and rural communities in the United States. During this time of active policy development at local, regional, national, and international levels, there is a critical need to understand how climate change will affect different populations. This report explores social vulnerability and the social dimensions of climate change to illustrate how policies can better meet the needs of these populations.

Governments, academia, nongovernmental organizations, and the media are rapidly generating articles, reports, and peer-reviewed publications related to climate-change science and global impacts. Current literature examines biophysical science that is related to the causes and effects of climate change. However, there is an increasing need to examine how diverse groups consider social issues that are related to climate change. In the same way, literature about natural hazards, disasters, and economic development illustrates disproportionate impacts on poor and socially vulnerable populations when catastrophic environmental, social, and economic events occur.

This literature synthesis presents information about social dimensions of climate change and explores how climate change literature addresses the contributions of, risks to, and opportunities for populations vulnerable to climate change in the United States and Canada. It is intended for policymakers, decisionmakers, and land managers in the United States who are involved in developing and implementing climate policies and plans.

This report begins by defining the literature for social vulnerability, equity, and other key concepts in the context of climate change, and by framing the climate issues explored within socially vulnerable urban and rural communities and American Indian and Alaska Native tribes in the United States. The report identifies specific populations at risk to climate change, explores the sectors in the United States that will be affected by climate change, and then present risks to socially vulnerable populations. Because a growing body of literature explores the impacts of climate change on American Indian and Alaska Native tribes, the report also explores the equity issues related to tribes and climate change, as well as the specific sectors that will affect tribes in the context of climate change.

Approach

The initial exploration of the literature reviewed definitions of social vulnerability, equity, and justice in the context of climate change as it relates to natural resource management and natural hazards and disasters. These definitions were used to guide the scope of the search into additional academic literature, government and nongovernmental publications and Web sites, and media reports related to socially vulnerable populations in the United States. The majority of literature reviewed for this synthesis was published from 2000 to 2009.

Geography and populations addressed—
The synthesis explores literature on how climate change is affecting indigenous peoples and socially vulnerable communities in urban and rural areas in the United States, particularly the Lower 48 States. The scope was narrowed in this way because the project, funded by the USDA Forest Service, is intended to provide land managers within the United States information about working with socially vulnerable populations within and adjacent to U.S. public lands. The synthesis also incorporates literature on climate change impacts to vulnerable populations in Canada and Alaska because of the prevalence of literature about these areas and the applicability of such information in the Lower 48 States. However, the report does not focus on these areas, because Alaska and Canada are addressed by a companion project.[1]

The primary populations examined in this synthesis include socially vulnerable urban and rural populations and indigenous populations. Socially vulnerable urban populations include communities of color (e.g., African Americans and Latinos-Latinas), single parents, low-income communities, the elderly, people with health constraints, and people historically marginalized in policymaking processes. Socially vulnerable rural populations include communities tied to surrounding natural resources for economy and jobs, in addition to the same communities of people listed for urban areas. Indigenous populations include American Indian tribes across the Lower 48 States, Alaska Natives, and First Nations in Canada.

Biophysical context of climate change—
An understanding of the biophysical effects of climate change is necessary when considering how social systems will be affected. The Intergovernmental Panel on Climate Change fourth assessment report describes how climate change presents the potential for rapid changes, such as more frequent extreme weather events, and subtle changes, such as changes in species distributions, plant-pollinator interactions, and water chemistry (IPCC 2007, Rosenzweig et al. 2008). This suggests that climate change presents the potential for increased exposure to rapid and subtle

---

[1] Draft report titled "Social vulnerability and equity in the context of climate change in Alaska and Canada. Synthesis of literature" On file with Valerie Barber, University of Alaska Fairbanks, 533 E Fireweed Ave. Palmer, AK 99645.

environmental changes and, in turn, rapid and subtle social, cultural, economic, and political changes.

Karl et al. (2009) described climate science and occurring and projected impacts at the global and national scales. Their work combines information about impacts on sectors at the national scale—water, energy supply and use, transportation, agriculture, ecosystems, human health, and society—with information about key impacts at regional scales. These scholars found that climate change poses the potential for increases in anticipated and unanticipated impacts on natural resources and society. Unanticipated impacts of increasing carbon dioxide concentrations include not only consequences of ecological changes, such as increases in ocean acidification, which diminishes the ability of sea creatures to build calcium carbonate shells, but also major shifts in wealth or technology. According to Karl et al. (2009), climate changes that are now occurring will continue and may shift in the future, presenting considerable challenges and uncertainty for adaptation. In contrast to the perceived steady environmental state of the past few centuries, Karl et al. (2009) asserted that society will not adapt to a new steady state, but rather to a continually and rapidly changing environment outside the range of past experience.

Climate changes will affect human society through impacts to basic needs: water, energy, housing, transportation, food, natural ecosystems, and health. Existing conditions, such as pollution, poverty, and an aging and growing population, can exacerbate climate impacts (Karl et al. 2009).

The Climate Change Science Program (Gamble et al. 2008) stressed the importance of considering climate impacts on human society in combination with nonclimatic factors, including existing issues and conditions—pollution, increasing immigrant and elderly populations, overburdened infrastructure, and increasing population in urban areas. They described the importance of considering climate impacts in relationship to geography, demographics, and complex social systems and links.

Literature reviewed—
The types of literature reviewed are listed below; the material reviewed generally covers the period from 2000 to 2009.

- Academic literature, including journal articles, conference proceedings, graduate student research, faculty presentations, and new, unpublished research.
- Popular press/popular media, including anecdotal information.
- Gray literature, including nongovernmental organization Web sites, blogs (Web logs), and discussion groups.

- Policy and government documents, such as the U.S. Department of Agriculture Forest Service climate change strategy and Congressional testimony.
- Non-climate-change literature, including publications related to natural hazards and natural resource management.

Literature that focused on socioeconomics, health and well-being, and access to services, resources, and decisionmaking processes was also examined. The synthesis examined literature that considered how climate impacts could affect different communities, such as children, the elderly, impoverished populations, migrants and immigrants, minority populations, people with mobility and cognitive constraints and chronic conditions, politically marginalized populations, single-head households, homeless men and women, natural-resource-dependent economies, and indigenous peoples. In addition, it focused on literature that considered how differences among populations may influence their vulnerability to climate impacts and their ability to respond, and how climate policy incorporates these differences. This synthesis draws from literature on climate impacts on urban and rural populations, particularly low-income and minority urban populations and natural-resource-dependent rural communities, and American Indian and Alaska Native tribes.

Literature on socially vulnerable urban and rural populations in the United States was found in several academic articles and reports and policy documents from governmental and nongovernmental organizations. After locating sources specific to African Americans, additional searches focused on African Americans and climate change effects and Latino-Latina populations and climate change effects.

The University of Oregon's database for social sciences includes the following search engines: Academic Search Premier, ArticleFirst, Web of Science, Sociological Abstracts, Public Affairs Information Service, Alternative Press Index, and Left Index. Search terms such as, "Latinos," "Latino populations," "Hispanics," "social vulnerability," "climate," and "climate change" were used in various combinations to find relevant literature. General Google searches offered more gray literature and nonprofit organization Web sites; Google Scholar offered academic articles, as did the University of Oregon database for social sciences. The National Latino Coalition on Climate Change Web site offered links to several of the resources incorporated herein. Much of the available literature focuses on communities of color and low-income populations, generally with reference to Latinos-Latinas and Hispanics included. The climate change literature focuses primarily on poverty and air quality concerns, as well as agricultural industry impacts and natural hazards and disasters.

To locate literature on indigenous peoples, academic publications, government reports, books, nonprofit publications, papers presented at meetings, and electronic news sources and blogs were searched. Reference lists in academic publications, government reports, books, and nonprofit publications offered leads to additional sources. The University of Oregon's library and Google were used to search for relevant academic journals, using keywords such as "indigenous populations" and "climate change" or "American Indians" and "climate change." Academic publications offered policy recommendations for considering equity in climate policy for indigenous populations. Few academic publications offered original research on climate impacts to indigenous peoples in the Lower 48 States.

Numerous articles, books, and nonprofit publications describe the climate risks to and adaptive capacities of indigenous peoples in Canada and Alaska and other vulnerable regions worldwide. These sources provide valuable context and insight on adaptive capacity, the role of traditional knowledge, ethics in integrating knowledge systems, equity in climate policy, and the range of climate impacts to tribal communities. Nonprofit publications and papers presented at meetings offered insight gained through climate research and planning projects with individual tribes and from tribe members experiencing climate impacts. Electronic news articles from sites including *News from Indian Country*, *Indian Country Today*, and E&E Publishing provide additional insight on climate risks. Using Google Alerts to track relevant articles on "tribes" and "climate change" in news, blogs, and Web sites, we located first-hand accounts that describe climate risks and impacts to tribes.

Because of time constraints, resources, scope, and approach, some segments of literature that contain important contributions on social dimensions of climate change in policy and program development are not included. For example, many aspects of social vulnerability in the international literature on climate change are not incorporated in this literature synthesis. The synthesis touches only briefly on race, gender, and youth issues, but there is a growing body of literature on these issues, particularly in an international context.

Areas of focus—

For human communities and the landscapes that sustain them, climate change poses risks to natural resources, institutions, infrastructure, and cultures. The degree to which communities are vulnerable to the effects of climate change depends on the nature of the effect as well as internal and external characteristics that comprise and influence human communities. A range of characteristics related to social vulnerability in rural and urban communities and within indigenous populations was explored. These areas include:

1. Equity and justice, including access to and participation in the processes and outcomes of policymaking, as well as ethical and legal issues related to responsibility among governments and populations to address climate change.
2. Culture and knowledge, including the impact of climate change on current and future generations, local and traditional knowledge, sense of place, and treaty rights and access to traditional resources.
3. Adaptive capacity, including relative power among populations, ability to address climate effects, and access to social processes and resources.
4. The role of race, ethnicity, and gender in climate change in the United States and Canada.

A range of natural and human sectors affected by climate change was also explored. Included were health, housing, transportation, economy and jobs, energy, climate-related hazards and disasters, water, natural resources (forestry, fish and wildlife, biodiversity, ecosystem services), food security, and land use.

Social Dimensions of Climate Change

Issues of climate ethics, vulnerability, equity, and justice relate to several questions: Who is to blame for the causes of climate change, and who bears responsibility for reducing greenhouse gas emissions and helping communities and populations around the world to prepare for the inevitable effects? On a global scale, many of the nations that bear the least responsibility for the causes of climate change are expected to suffer the most significant consequences. Many of these same countries (primarily developing nations and poor communities) hold the most promise for reducing greenhouse gas emissions through the production of renewable energy and opportunities to sequester carbon.

Questions related to climate change responsibility provide an important frame when examining climate change and social vulnerability. This is especially true as climate change policies begin to provide incentives to industrialized nations and higher capacity communities to engage in and profit from carbon-reduction programs.

This section draws on the literature to provide definitions and considerations for social vulnerability, equity, and justice in the context of climate change impacts and policies. Although the remainder of this synthesis focuses on populations in the United States, this section of definitions draws from international literature to provide a more thorough understanding of all facets of social vulnerability and dimensions of equity. Policymakers and planners can consider how climate change impacts and policies might differently affect populations based on age, gender, ability, health, citizenship status, race, class, scale, capacity, sovereignty, and geography. They can consider how these populations may access, participate in, and receive the outputs and outcomes of climate policies and plans.

Social Vulnerability

Social vulnerability provides an overarching lens through which to view the potentially disproportionate impacts that climate change may have on communities and individuals worldwide. The social vulnerability perspective points to the types of populations that might have limited access to information and resources and suffer increased impacts from extreme events based on limited capacity. To clarify the social dimensions of vulnerability, definitions of social vulnerability are presented in the context of natural hazards and climate change.

Literature focused on natural hazards provides a number of definitions of social vulnerability within the disaster context. Wisner et al. (2004: 11) defined vulnerability broadly in relation to natural hazards as "the characteristics of a person or group and their situation that influence their capacity to anticipate, cope with, resist and recover from the impact of a natural hazard (an extreme natural event or process)." Cutter and Finch (2008) defined social vulnerability as a measure of both the sensitivity of a population to natural hazards and its ability to respond to and recover from the impacts of hazards. The United Nations Development Programme (2000) defined it as "...the degree to which societies or socioeconomic groups are affected by stresses and hazards, whether brought about by external forces or intrinsic factors—internal and external—that negatively impact the social cohesion of a country" (UNDP 2000).

A number of authors suggested indicators for measuring and understanding vulnerability, including levels of income, unemployment, pension contributions, illiteracy and malnutrition among children (LegCo Secretariat 2005), livelihood resilience, self protection, societal protection, social capital, class or income group, gender, ethnicity, type of state, civil society, and science and technology (Cannon 2000).

Researchers of disasters and natural hazards suggested that the roots of vulnerability extend to social structures and settlement and development patterns; these constructs affect access to resources, power, information, and networks. Like disasters (Fothergill and Peek 2004), the effects of climate change and climate policy could reveal and exacerbate social inequities if decisionmakers take no action to address them. Understanding the relationships and dimensions of socially vulnerable populations will facilitate the formulation of policies to reduce vulnerability among these populations (LegCo Secretariat 2005).

Vulnerability and its social dimensions can be considered specifically in the context of climate change. The Intergovernmental Panel on Climate Change (IPCC), an international, scientific body set up by the World Meteorological Organization and United Nations Environment Programme, defines vulnerability as "the degree to which a system is susceptible to, or unable to cope with, adverse effects of climate change, including variability and extremes… Vulnerability is a function of the character, magnitude and rate of climate change and variation to which the system is exposed, its sensitivity, and its adaptive capacity" (Parry et al. 2007: 883).

Burton et al. (2002) assessed the first round of adaptation studies conducted under the United Nations Framework Convention on Climate Change and described how research on adaptation (which refers to preparing, responding, and coping with the effects of climate change) has evolved from a consideration of mitigation policy (aimed at reducing greenhouse gas emissions) to a stand-alone policy prerogative. Burton et al. (2002) described climate vulnerability as a function of impacts and adaptation. Impacts result from a system's sensitivity and exposure to climate-related stimuli; adaptation results from a system's capacity to adapt and its willingness or ability to apply adaptive capacity to reduce vulnerability (Burton et al. 2002).

How vulnerability is defined in the context of climate change will affect the factors considered and included in climate policy (Burton et al. 2002). Examining how vulnerability is socially and spatially differentiated across populations and scales of decisionmaking will help illustrate the implications of climate change and climate change policy on socially vulnerable populations in the United States and international community.

Adaptive capacity and local institutions—

Gamble et al. (2008) described the need to consider the role of human and social capital in determining vulnerability to climate impacts. They suggested that countries with greater human capital—knowledge, skills, and experience—could be less vulnerable to climate change because of their increased capacity to address it. In addition, they described the need to consider social capital—trust, relationships, support networks, and knowledge transfer systems—in identifying climate vulnerability. They suggested that human and social capital can contribute to a community's ability to address climate change through coping and responses, whereas a lack of capital can leave individuals isolated and at greater risk of exposure to impacts such as extreme heat waves.

The literature suggests that local institutions do have a role to play in implementing climate adaptation and building adaptive capacity for populations vulnerable to climate change. Gamble et al. (2008) considered the role of institutions to be rules, social norms, and systems that guide human behavior, such as past land use development, existing environmental laws, and legal rights and building codes. They described how institutions past and present affect society's ability to respond to changes, and they provided examples of institutions. Ogden and Innes (2009) described factors that limit adaptive capacity in local institutions and networks in their study of 30 forest practitioners in the rural Yukon region of Canada.

> Family-level resistance to lifestyle change, **poor access to local and traditional knowledge (there is a rich supply but it is not easily accessed)**, and the lack of identified markets for local forest products were also identified as potentially reducing adaptive capacity in the region [Ogden and Innes 2009, emphasis added].

Agrawal (2008: 5) focused on the role of local institutions in adaptation to climate change; he defined local institutions as "humanly created formal and informal mechanisms that shape social and individual expectations, interactions, and behavior." Agrawal (2008: 3) took note of local institutions because he believed that climate change will disproportionately affect disadvantaged populations, and "local institutions centrally influence how different social groups gain access to and are able to use assets and resources" that might be important in adapting to climate change. He listed some of the functions of local institutions, such as "information gathering and dissemination, resource mobilization and allocation, skills development and capacity building, providing leadership, and relating to other decision-makers and institutions" (Agrawal 2008: 28). Agrawal suggested that the adaptation practices that many institutions (both formal and informal) have employed in the past may not be enough to cope with the changes that are linked with climate change.

Agrawal noted also that disadvantaged populations can benefit from institutions with "proactive approaches that address social processes leading rural poor into vulnerable conditions, and structural inequalities that are often at the root of social-environmental vulnerabilities" (2008: 17).

Wall and Marzall (2006) described the number of social networks in rural areas, the human potential to help in emergency conditions, and human resources available. Human resources, the authors suggested, include communities with educated populations capable of "productive activity" that "may have a better chance of acting on climate risk management strategies, coping with severe weather events and seeking out potential benefits from altered conditions" (Wall and Marzall 2006: 382). They also noted that this productive population is important in rural areas because it may need to take on more burdens during extreme events such as floods, when others in the community, including the young and elderly, could suffer disproportionately and weaken the community's resilience. Wall and Marzall (2006) suggested that social networks are important in times of stress to facilitate collective action and for communication. The authors noted specific instances, including recent ice storms and forest fires, in which people helping people was as important as if not more important than emergency services.

Social and spatial scales of vulnerability—
Ford et al. (2006) focused on integrating social, physical, and health sciences and local and indigenous knowledge in climate change vulnerability and adaptation research, particularly at the local level, for the Inuit in the Arctic region of Canada. Concerning the Inuit in Igloolik, Nunavut, Canada (but applicable to communities worldwide), they suggested that the interaction between human communities and landscapes from local to global scales will shape climate change effects.

Liverman and Merideth (2002) suggested that improved climate information could assist decisionmakers in addressing climate impacts and understanding how impacts could be socially differentiated. They focused on describing the relationship between society and climate in the Southwest to provide a frame for the regional climate assessment project—Climate Assessment for the Southwest. In considering the relationships among society and climate and vulnerability, they reviewed five elements: demography, economy, land, water, and institutions and values. They suggest the importance of considering social context and the differentiation of vulnerability across the population.

Many factors at several scales need to be included in a comprehensive contextual analysis for regional climate assessments, such as socioeconomic conditions and trends, resource distribution and use, institutions, as well as relevant cultural traditions and values. Context also might include an analysis of the major networks of power that control decision-making and information flow, and of the nature of integration of the region into a national or global economy [Liverman and Merideth 2002: 202].

Gamble et al. (2008) focused on the impacts of climate change on human health, settlements, and welfare. They considered how climate impacts will affect human society and how society may adapt; they offered common themes and research recommendations. Gamble et al. (2008) asserted that research on climate change and vulnerable populations is underdeveloped and cited connections made between natural hazards and vulnerable populations for context. In considering indicators for well-being, Gamble et al. (2008) described the importance of acknowledging that communities will experience climate impacts at local and regional levels. Communities and regions will differ in geographic and biological vulnerability to climate impacts. Although vulnerability analyses tend to be done on a regional scale, vulnerability exists at finer scales (Gamble et al. 2008).

In addition, Gamble et al. (2008) suggested that people within communities will experience climate impacts differently; some people may be more at risk to climate impacts and related stresses, including the poor, the elderly, people living alone, people in poor health, indigenous populations, and people with limited power and rights. They suggested that planners and decisionmakers take into account the social and spatial differentiation of climate impacts and ability to adapt.

Gamble et al. (2008) also acknowledged the span of impacts across jurisdictions and geographies, particularly the transmission of communicable diseases through legal and illegal tourism and immigration. Climate impacts—economic, social, and health—are not and will not be confined to specific geographic or political boundaries or times. Hurricane Katrina in New Orleans and surrounding communities is an example.

> As Hurricane Katrina made clear, impacts felt in one community ripple throughout the region and nation. Many of the persons made homeless in New Orleans resettled in Baton Rouge, Lafayette, and Houston, creating stresses on those communities. Vulnerable groups migrate from stricken areas to more hospitable ones, taking their health, economic, and educational needs and problems with them across both national and state lines [Gamble et al. 2008: 123].

Gamble et al. (2008) asserted that populations in certain geographic regions may be more vulnerable to human health and welfare impacts associated with climate change; geographic regions may be vulnerable because of their baseline climate, elevation, proximity to coasts or rivers, natural resource availability, and infrastructure connected to natural resources such as drinking water wells. They suggested that human populations in low-lying coastal areas, such as the Gulf Coast region, are particularly vulnerable to climate-related health impacts.

Regional climate vulnerability in the United States—
There are numerous government and academic sources of information on the physical effects of climate change in different regions throughout the United States. Some of the literature reviewed for this synthesis presents information on social aspects of vulnerability from a geographic perspective. Examples include extreme heat events leading to deaths (particularly in major cities and associated with urban heat island effects), vulnerability among people without home air conditioning in the Great Lakes Region and western arid settlements, water

scarcity among populations in the West, Southwest, and Great Plains, and risks to coastal communities in the Southeast. Other examples are thawing ground that destabilizes transportation and buildings, prompting needs to rebuild in or relocate communities, and economic and cultural impacts to indigenous communities in Alaska (Gamble et al. 2008, Karl et al. 2009).

Equity and Justice

Studies of the procedural and distributive dimensions of equity provide a foundation for much of the discussion on climate equity and climate justice in the literature.

Climate change equity—

To integrate equity into climate change mitigation and adaptation policy and planning, it is important to understand its dimensions and how they relate to policymaking. In the context of climate policy, Ikeme (2003) suggested looking at equity in the distribution of climate change impacts, responsibility, and costs and benefits, and in the procedures of drafting, implementing, and monitoring climate policies and plans.

Through an analysis of international climate mitigation policy mechanisms—"the new carbon economy"—and a case study of application in Chiapas, Mexico, Brown and Corbera (2003) explored three elements of equity: access to markets and forests, legitimacy in decisionmaking and institutions, and outcomes. Their article focuses on the Kyoto Protocol and the potential of its mechanisms to provide incentives to natural resource managers for sustainable development; furthermore, pilot forest project results may influence guidelines for offset projects in the next round of Kyoto. Equity in access considers a person's ability to engage and participate and the factors involved, including information, knowledge, communication, property rights, access rules, and the way different institutions operate at different scales. Equity in procedure considers institutions and decisionmaking, how projects and rules operate, and the ability of all stakeholders to participate in the project. Finally, equity in outcomes considers how projects affect individuals and how costs and benefits are distributed among them as a result of access and decisionmaking (Brown and Corbera 2003).

Paavola and Adger (2006) explored social justice in the context of climate change adaptation decisions at the international and national levels. They considered to what extent the existing "climate change regime"—international rules, norms, decisionmaking processes, and procedures for developing policies or "adaptive responses"—addresses procedural and distributive justice dilemmas. In climate adaptation policy, Paavola and Adger (2006) identified equity in four areas:

(1) the procedural dimensions of climate change adaptation planning and decision-making; (2) the responsibility of developed countries for climate change impacts; (3) the amount of that assistance that developed countries should provide to developing countries for adaptation; and (4) the distribution of that amount among developing countries.

Climate justice—

Climate justice, a term that combines social and environmental justice in the context of climate change, advocates for equity in climate policies and plans and their outputs and outcomes.

The Environmental Justice and Climate Change Initiative (EJCC) is a consensus-based coalition of climate and environmental justice, policy, religious, and advocacy organizations in the United States. The EJCC works to educate individuals, communities, and policymakers about the environmental and social justice implications of climate change at the international and national levels. It also ensures the accountability, transparency, and inclusion of marginalized voices in the climate policy dialogue. The EJCC defines climate justice as "the fair treatment of all people and freedom from discrimination with the creation of policies and projects that address climate change and the systems that create climate change and perpetuate discrimination" (EJCC 2009).

Climate justice considers how the people most vulnerable to climate change are involved in the development of policies, the language used to address them, and, ultimately, how they are affected by the outputs and outcomes of climate policies and plans. Because these policies and plans are currently being drafted at local, national, and international levels, it is important to identify the dimensions of equity and justice that need to be addressed.

Macchi et al. (2008) considered the vulnerability to climate change of indigenous and traditional peoples worldwide; the implications of climate change for indigenous and traditional peoples (particularly the sociocultural risks); and the adaptation, mitigation, and policy strategies to address climate change and protect traditional and indigenous peoples. The report's motivation is to offer information to help ensure that climate policy and programs incorporate sociocultural considerations. Macchi et al. (2008) also suggested that without addressing equity worldwide, indigenous, low-income, and rural resource-based communities could be disproportionately affected by the impacts of climate change because of their vulnerability to current and future stresses.

Crump (2008) focused on climate change adaptation in the Arctic and small-island developing states (SIDS) and other issues in the circumpolar region, including human security and co-management. In an article featured in *Indigenous*

Affairs, Crump expressed insight about the effect of climate change on indigenous peoples of the Arctic and SIDS, two geographic areas most vulnerable to climate change in which the most vulnerable populations are indigenous peoples. Crump (2008) described the Many Strong Voices Programme, which is intended to provide awareness of climate change impacts on indigenous peoples. The article described the programme's focus on vulnerability and adaptation research that integrates scientific and traditional knowledge. It emphasized knowledge sharing to help people develop appropriate adaptation strategies, outreach to expose the impacts and capacity of communities in the Arctic and SIDS, and advocacy to ensure global climate policy discussions include consideration for the vulnerability of SIDS and the Arctic. The article suggested that the actions and efforts that are taking place in communities in the Arctic and SIDS are important for the rest of the world as it prepares for climate change and for worldwide communities as they consider their adaptive capacity to address climate change.

In addition, if some communities are unable to act to address climate change because they lack resources or opportunities to engage, Crump (2008) suggested that this will affect the ability of all communities to address climate change.

> The interventions at all levels in which indigenous peoples exist must be based on an understanding on the part of the promoters that there is a need for equity and on the recognition that their own prosperity will be unsustainable if it locks others out or displaces other people and that, for them to gain, others do not have to lose [Crump 2008: 41].

Vulnerability, Equity, and Justice in Climate Policy

International and U.S. climate policy—
The international climate policy discussion predates the 1992 United Nations Framework Convention on Climate Change (UNFCCC), the first international, legal agreement developed to address climate change. Since then, developing and developed nations have negotiated their roles in addressing climate change. These negotiations have spurred considerable thought and literature about the dimensions of equity involved in developing climate policy and assigning roles and responsibilities.

Equity is an important consideration in climate change mitigation and adaptation policy. International climate policy discussion has focused on mitigation or the reduction of greenhouse gas emissions. Although some developing countries have sought assistance for adaptation since the beginning, as awareness and observations of climate change effects have grown, discussion has expanded to focus also on adaptation, or reducing vulnerability to climate change. Today, discussion persists on how to calculate responsibility for emissions and emissions reductions, and to use revenue from mitigation strategies to address climate change adaptation. Although uncertainty remains about the degree of impacts, enough evidence exists to heighten the urgency for action to reduce greenhouse gas emissions and reduce vulnerability to impacts (Parry et al. 2007).

A history of distrust, inconsistency, and inequity—
Inequality in environmental protection policy has created distrust and divergent perspectives among developed and developing countries (Parks and Roberts 2006, Tsosie 2007). Within international climate policy discussions, distrust has slowed progress in addressing climate change and assigning roles and responsibilities. Yet, divergent perspectives persist as a result of inequitable access to and consideration in policymaking and planning. In an analysis of the UNFCCC, the Kyoto Protocol, the Clean Development Mechanism, the Stern Review, and the Intergovernmental Panel on Climate Change's fourth assessment report, Macchi et al. (2008) suggested that although the documents acknowledge the disproportionate impacts of climate change on the most vulnerable communities, these communities are not considered consistently in adaptation and mitigation strategies.

> Even though these documents agree that the costs of climate change are going to fall inequitably on the world's poorest and most disadvantaged communities including traditional and indigenous peoples, the communities discussed almost exclusively live in developed countries, i.e. in North America, Europe, Australia and New Zealand and the Polar Regions. The majority of traditional and indigenous peoples, who live in the tropical developing world, get very little or no consideration. Furthermore, while all the analysed documents put their emphasis on monetary, knowledge and technology transfer from developed to developing countries, traditional and indigenous peoples' own coping and adaptive strategies are hardly recognized [Macchi et al. 2008: 4].

Parks and Roberts (2006) traced the issue of inequality in environmental protection policy from the 1972 United Nations conference on Human Environment through the signing of the UNFCC in 1992. Parks and Roberts stated that although industrialized nations committed to "taking the lead" in reducing emissions, "rich nations began to backpedal on their promise of massive technology transfer and technical assistance to the developing world" (Parks and Roberts 2006: 338).

Distributing responsibility, impacts, costs, and benefits—
Integrating equity requires acknowledging differences in responsibility for climate change and its effects, costs, and benefits. Parks and Roberts (2006) articulated the differences among developed and developing countries in contributions to greenhouse gas emissions.

> With only 4 percent of the world's population, the U.S. is responsible for over 20 percent of all global emissions. That can be compared to 136 developing countries that together are only responsible for 24 percent of global emissions.... Overall, the richest 20 percent of the world's population is responsible for over 60 percent of its current emissions of greenhouse gases. That figure surpasses 80 percent if past contributions to the problem are considered [Parks and Roberts 2006: 341].

Ikeme (2003) suggested that the dilemma about addressing the distributive issues of climate change (impacts, responsibility, costs, and benefits) stems from different uses of environmental justice in the North and South. Whereas the North focuses on economics and efficiency in addressing climate change impacts, the South focuses on equality and distribution of responsibility for emissions and impacts. Ikeme (2003) maintained that the differences in interpreting environmental justice lead to opposing and incomplete proposals for addressing climate change. The North has favored the "grandfathering rule," and the South prefers "equal rights per capita entitlements." Ikeme (2003) suggested that the Kyoto protocol's emissions cap, based on 1990 levels, reflects the interpretation favored by the North. However, although the interpretations of the North and South differ regarding ethics, they result in a similar conclusion: "Greater burden for climate protection should be borne by the North, and North-South transfer of resources should be used to facilitate climate protection and adaptation in the South" (Ikeme 2003: 203).

Paavola and Adger (2006: 595) presented four principles for addressing justice dilemmas related to climate change: "avoiding dangerous climate change," "forward-looking responsibility," "putting the most vulnerable first," and "equal participation of all." They emphasized the importance of participation by developing countries in the determination of adaptation decisions. The authors recognized differences that must be addressed when international norms, rules, and decisionmaking processes are applied at national and particularly local levels, where contributions to climate change are negligible, but where impacts will be felt the most.

In a report for the Pew Center on Equity and Global Climate Change, Clausen and McNeilly (1998) discussed what constitutes a fair response to climate change. They suggested three criteria for determining the role nations should play in climate change mitigation: (1) responsibility for the emissions that can cause climate change, (2) standard of living (or the ability to pay for climate change mitigation), and (3) the opportunity to reduce emissions. Clausen and McNeilly recommended the creation of three tiers of nations that must act, should act, and could act, based directly on who is responsible for emissions, has the resources to act, and the opportunities to reduce emissions now and in the future. In their report, Clausen and McNeilly (1998: 2) proposed five principles of equity to guide international policy negotiations for climate change:

1. All nations should be able to maintain or improve standards of living under a global climate change mitigation regime. Consequently, climate change mitigation should focus on alternative, low-carbon development paths that do not reduce economic growth.

2. More broadly, the outcome of UNFCCC negotiations should not undermine or hinder progress toward the goal of sustainable development.

3. The countries most responsible for greenhouse gas concentrations in the atmosphere should be leaders in the effort to reduce emissions.

4. All nations should work to the best of their abilities—or with help from other countries—to reduce emissions either absolutely or relative to business-as-usual trajectories.

5. The world should take advantage of emission-reduction opportunities where they exist.

In part, determining a safe, maximum standard will affect the distribution of climate responsibility and costs. Paavola and Adger (2006: 602) stressed that the highest priority in climate policy is determining and agreeing on a "safe maximum standard" of global greenhouse gas emissions, "a level that does not surpass the capacity of natural systems, food production systems, and economic systems to adapt." They suggested that costs in climate policy can be considered in relation to emissions targets and that the mechanisms that are implemented to reach those targets, such as a cap-and-trade system or a carbon tax, can also be considered to facilitate adaptation. However, each relies in part on allocating responsibility.

Vulnerable Populations at Risk to Climate Change in the United States

Low-Income and Minority Populations

For urban populations, the literature focuses on the distributive effects of climate change on low-income and minority populations and introduces new concepts into the social vulnerability lexicon. Morello-Frosch et al. (2009: 5) explored the specific vulnerabilities to climate change of those in the climate gap, which they define as "the disproportionate and unequal impact the climate crisis has on people of color and the poor." They suggested that as energy, food, and water prices continue to rise (especially water prices in the Western United States), the spending gap will grow because low-income families spend a larger proportion of their income on food, energy, and other household needs.

> A program implemented to cut carbon dioxide emissions by 15 percent would cost 3.3 percent of the average income of households in the lowest income bracket as opposed to only 1.7 percent of the average income of the households in the top income bracket (Orzag 2007).

Karl et al. (2009) supported Morello-Frosch's definition of the climate gap and suggested that people with financial resources possess greater capacity to adapt to impacts. The poor have less access and capacity to adapt and, as a result of impacts, could experience permanent dislocation and the loss of social networks and support systems. Karl et al. (2009) maintained that vulnerability is greater for those who have few resources and choices; the very young, the very old, the sick, and the poor are most at risk from climate impacts. The authors pointed out that these groups make up different proportions of the population in different locations.

Shonkoff et al. (2009) and Cordova et al. (2006) agreed that the consequences of climate change will likely have a disproportionate impact on vulnerable communities. Shonkoff et al. (2009) explored the vulnerability of low-income populations to extreme weather events and suggested that low-income populations are underinsured and therefore more at risk to the impacts of extreme weather events. Liverman and Merideth (2002) showed that the poor are often more vulnerable to extreme events such as drought because they have less access to financial or informational resources and lower or limited insurance coverage.

African American communities—

The climate change literature stresses impacts on African Americans. African Americans, who make up only 13 percent of the U.S. population, on average are responsible for nearly 20 percent less emission of greenhouse gases than are non-Hispanic Whites per capita (Hoerner and Robinson 2008). Yet, like so many other marginalized populations who are less responsible for the causes of climate change, African Americans are more vulnerable to its effects on health, housing, the economy, and culture in their own communities. They are also more vulnerable to higher energy bills, unemployment, and recessions caused by global energy price shocks (Hoerner and Robinson (2008). Hoerner and Robinson (2008) based their findings found that African Americans are and will be disproportionately affected by climate change based on the following factors:

- **Public health**: Climate change will result in increased heat waves and the potential for increased heat-related deaths. Currently, African American heat-related deaths are 150 to 200 percent those of non-Hispanic Whites. Climate change will cause increased air pollution and the potential for increased respiratory health problems, including asthma. Currently, 71 percent of African Americans live in counties in violation of federal air pollution standards (compared to 58 percent of non-Hispanic Whites). In addition, 78 percent of African Americans live within 30 miles of a coal-fired powerplant (compared to 56 percent of Whites), and African Americans have a thirty-six percent higher rate of incidents of asthma than Whites.

- **Energy**: Climate change will result in increased energy rates and increased fluctuation in oil prices. Currently, African Americans spend 30 percent more of their income on energy compared to Whites.

- **Food security**: Increased food costs and decreased food availability will result from climate change. The potential impacts of climate change include more frequent and more intense extreme weather events, which could damage crops and affect crop yields; and climate mitigation strategies, such as biofuel crops, could also affect food crop yields.

- **Economy and jobs**: Climate change will result in increases in health problems and associated need for health insurance. Currently, 20 percent of African Americans lack health insurance, about twice the rate of Whites. Climate change will affect jobs and income, which for an African American household averages 57 percent less than that for Whites.

Hoerner and Robinson (2008) also described how proposed policies to address climate change, including cap-and-trade, cap-and-dividend, and the climate asset plan, will have differing effects on sectors of the population. In particular, they suggested that a cap-and-dividend system would benefit everyone except populations with the highest incomes. The climate asset plan, which would rely on energy efficiency to mitigate increased energy costs, would benefit everyone, including African Americans and other low-income populations by about twice as much as the cap-and-dividend system.

Latino-Latina communities—
The National Survey of Hispanic Voters on Environmental Issues (Bendixen and Associates 2008) stated that, in addition to toxic air and water, climate change is the most important environmental problem facing Latino families.

A National Hispanic Environmental Council and Clean the Air factsheet (2010) suggested that climate change poses risks to the economy and jobs, health, and well-being of Latinos because of the number of Latino families living in poverty and lacking access to services, resources, health insurance, and adequate housing. The factsheet suggests that living in poverty and lacking English language proficiency increase the vulnerability of Latinos to health risks associated with natural hazards, disasters, and air pollution. The factsheet also describes the agricultural industry's vulnerability to climate change and the resulting vulnerability of Latinos, whom the industry employs in large numbers and who spend a larger portion of their income on food compared to non-Latino Whites.

Keating (2004), in a science-based report, compiled information on the health effects of air pollution on Latinos. Keating suggested that language barriers and poverty contribute to Latinos' vulnerability to the effects of poor air quality and increases in ozone and natural hazards associated with climate change. Poverty decreases housing options and access to health care for Latinos. The National Hispanic Environmental Council factsheet similarly stated that climate change increases the vulnerability of Latinos to develop acute and chronic illnesses (such as asthma) from exposure to toxic air. It pointed out that 72 percent of the Latino population in the United States lives in areas that fail to meet federal air pollution standards and 70 percent lives in areas that fail to meet federal standards for ozone.

Keating (2004) suggested that health-related issues that affect Latinos are undocumented or under-documented because national data collection and research often exclude Latinos and Hispanics, and health researchers who inform national policy lack information regarding Latinos.

Undocumented migrants—
Liverman and Merideth (2002) suggested that undocumented migrants in the Southwest could be disproportionately vulnerable to health impacts associated with climate change. They specifically described the vulnerability of colonias (rural settlements along the U.S.-Mexico border) to vector-borne diseases, including hanta virus, which has been linked to climate changes in the past.

The California Rural Legal Assistance Foundation, as cited by Liverman and Merideth (2002), stated that more undocumented migrants are crossing from Mexico into Arizona and New Mexico because of tighter border controls in Texas and California. Every summer, migrants are found dead or dehydrated from the desert heat and lack of water.

Suburban Poor

The literature offers perspectives on the suburban poor in the context of social vulnerability and climate change. Gamble et al. (2008) stressed the importance of considering the people living in poverty in suburbs, a trend referred to as "the suburbanization of poverty." The report states that many suburban poor live in the Nation's first suburbs—older, inner-ring neighborhoods developed in the 1950s and 1960s. Gamble et al. suggested (citing Puentes and Warren 2006) that these neighborhoods have unique challenges that are different from inner cities and newer, growing communities. They include concentrated immigrant and elderly populations, outdated buildings and homes, and lack of consideration in federal or state policy.

Similarly, in their summary of the science and impacts of climate change on the United States, Karl et al. (2009) suggested that location and circumstances influence social vulnerability. The authors refer to the case of Hurricane Katrina in which the poor and elderly experienced disproportionate impacts.

Issues associated with access and proximity to information, resources, and services are raised in the literature on urban populations and the poor more generally. Liverman and Merideth (2002) suggested that inadequate housing, water supplies, and health care can also make the poor more vulnerable to vector-borne and waterborne diseases and other climate-related illnesses.

Karl et al. (2009) added that the very young, the elderly, and other vulnerable populations make up large proportions of rural communities in the Great Plains region. These populations are more at risk to the health impacts of climate change than urban communities because they have less access to health care.

Rural, Resource-Based Communities

Rural, resource-based communities are generally considered to be those communities surrounded by public or private lands that are dominated by natural resources, including forests, rangelands, and agriculture. The livelihoods of these communities are tied to natural resources.

Climate change poses increased risks to rural communities that rely on natural resources, such as forests, cropland and rangeland, waterways, and open spaces

(Eriksen et al. 2007, Karl et al. 2009). Because of their connection to the land and the potential for climate change to impact natural resources and disrupt ecosystems and seasons, rural livelihoods and well-being are disproportionately vulnerable to climate change (Davidson et al. 2003, Liverman and Merideth 2002).

Davidson et al. (2003) described the increased risk climate change poses to forest-based communities in Canada because these communities share proximity and strong linkages to climate-sensitive forest environments. As a result, the values at risk for households in these forest-based communities are likely higher than for other social groupings. Keller Jensen (2009) described the specific implications of climate change on vulnerable populations in rural areas in the United States. Rural communities are part of a group of climate-vulnerable populations because they have a large proportion of people who are less economically or physically capable of adapting to climate change. These include seniors, the poor, and those employed in climate-sensitive sectors.

Socially vulnerable populations in rural areas, including the young, elderly, people of low income, and communities of color, face disproportionate risks in the face of climate change because of already limited access to health services, emergency services, and employment opportunities (Keller Jensen 2009).

Equity issues are raised in the literature related to rural populations. Eriksen et al. (2007) showed that some actions to address climate change potentially can have negative impacts on rural populations. Not all types of climate-related adjustments will reduce the vulnerability of the poor, and, in some cases, could even increase the vulnerability of some groups. Likewise, adaptation measures, such as building dams and irrigation systems to stabilize water supply, may disadvantage some groups. As an example, Eriksen et al. (2007) pointed to those whom, as a result of a new infrastructure, lose access to important water resources that they use in coping with drought.

Although the review does not focus specifically on the policy advocacy literature, some articles did present policy recommendations to reduce climate impacts and strengthen procedural and distributive aspects of equity in climate policy for vulnerable populations. Focusing on rural areas in an international context, Locatelli et al. (2008) recommended that populations that are inextricably linked to forests for their well-being (e.g., forest products, clean water, or ecotourism) should be involved in the management of these forests, especially given the changes that will come with climate change. The authors also noted that stakeholders who manage natural resources often have few (if any) links to those who benefit from or bear the consequences of the loss from ecosystem services.

Climate Change Impacts on Vulnerable Populations by Sector

Public Health

Air pollution—

Climate change is expected to exacerbate health and safety concerns related to air pollution, including air pollution from industrial sources and in urban areas. Temperature increases and associated urban, heat-island effects and mitigation policies such as cap-and-trade systems could exacerbate existing issues. Ash et al. (2009) explored the uneven distribution of air pollution in the United States by mapping industrial air pollution across the country, considering who is exposed to the dirtiest air and the industrial companies that are contributing to the pollution. They relied on information from the Environmental Protection Agency's Risk Screening Environmental Indicators project. The authors suggested that low-income people and communities of color, including Latinos, African Americans, Asian Americans, and Native Americans, bear the most exposure to toxic air. Ash et al. (2009) noted that affected communities differ by race, ethnicity, and class across the country, but all three factors deserve consideration in addressing the disparities that exist. However, they pointed out that many studies demonstrate the disproportionate exposure of communities of color across all income levels.

Climate impacts resulting from stagnant air masses and ground-level ozone could increase poor air quality conditions in the United States (Karl et al. 2009). Ozone exposure compromises lung function and exacerbates respiratory diseases such as asthma. For this reason, children, outdoor workers, and athletes are more vulnerable. In addition, Californians currently are exposed to the worst air quality in the nation—air quality that wildfires (already increasing owing to warming) could further degrade (Karl et al. 2009).

Morello-Frosch et al. (2009) maintained that although air pollution is not directly related to climate change, the effects of climate change will worsen California's already big problem with air pollution. This will lead to more illnesses, and those more vulnerable to illness will be most affected. This is consistent with the concerns raised by Gamble et al. (2008) that people with chronic medical conditions or certain biologically acquired or genetic factors could be more sensitive to climate-related health effects. These might include an increased sensitivity to heat in people with chronic heart conditions and an increased sensitivity to air pollution in people with genetic conditions. The authors also noted that socioeconomic status affects vulnerability, considering its influence on exposure to toxins, nutrition, and access to resources and health care. Few (2006) described the social differentiation of health risks in the context of climate change, particularly during natural hazards, as a function of the coping capacity of individuals and health systems and institutions.

Davidson et al. (2003) stated that smoke from forest fires and potential heat waves could cause a problem for rural, forest-based communities in northern Canada. Thick smoke has led to increased chronic obstructive pulmonary disease (COPD) in community elders in rural northern California (Jungwirth 2009).

Urban heat island effect—

The urban heat island effect is a pocket of higher temperatures around urban areas caused by dark-colored materials in roads, buildings, and other structures that absorb heat and do not allow it to dissipate at the same rate as soil, grass, forests, and other less-industrial materials (Oke 1973 in Morello-Frosch et al. 2009). Several authors suggested that heat islands affect low-income urban neighborhoods and communities of color more because they are often segregated in the inner city (Schultz et al. 2002, Williams and Collins 2001 as cited by Morello-Frosch et al. 2009). Others focused on the disproportionate health impacts on the young and elderly associated with urbanization and increased heat island effects (Liverman and Merideth 2002). Karl et al. (2009) suggested that extreme heat waves are projected to increase, and the aging U.S. population increases the number of elderly people more vulnerable to projected heat waves. Karl et al. (2009) also pointed out the increasing prevalence of diabetes and obesity in the United States and that diabetics are at greater risk to hot weather and heat waves and the resulting health impacts, including kidney stones and heat exhaustion.

Heat and poor air quality health impacts are connected and increase the vulnerability of population sectors that are at risk to both, such as children (Karl et al. 2009). The formation of ground-level ozone occurs under hot and stagnant conditions that accompany heat waves. This results in interactions among risk factors that are likely to increase as climate change continues (Karl et al. 2009). Morello-Frosch et al. (2009) maintained that people with low incomes and people of color are less likely to have access to air conditioning, which disproportionately increases the risk of illness and death related to heat. Cordova et al. (2006) supported this finding and suggested that warmer weather is expected to affect California especially hard, as well as particularly vulnerable communities in urban areas and those with outdoor employment.

Also focusing on California, Basu and Ostro (2009) examined populations vulnerable to increases in ambient air temperature across a nine-county area. They identified high-risk populations as the elderly who have some specific preexisting disease or who take certain medications (i.e., beta-blockers, major tranquilizers, and diuretics), people with lower socioeconomic status (e.g., those engaged in outdoor occupations), and socially isolated populations (e.g., those who live alone, especially on higher floors of apartment buildings). The California Climate Change Public Health Impacts Assessment and Response Collaborative (2007) noted that 64 percent of the heat wave deaths in California in 2006 were in economically depressed areas. They suggested that air conditioning could decrease heat exposure, but homes in lower income areas are less likely to have air conditioning.

Economy and Jobs

The majority of jobs in sectors that will likely be significantly affected by climate change, such as agriculture and tourism, are held by low-income people of color [Morello-Frosch et al. 2009: 15].

Cordova et al. (2006) noted that the tourism industry is a major employer of low-income residents and people of color. The effects of climate change are expected to burden the tourism sector heavily, with people traveling less and the number of health problems increasing. Therefore, people of color will "bear a disproportionate burden of any economic hardships associated with disruptions in tourism caused by climate change" (Cordova et al. 2006: 67). The authors also suggested that many low-income residents and people of color do not have access to health insurance, which limits their ability to recover from health problems associated with the effects of climate change, thus causing them to lose money because of missed work days and potential health-care bills.

Environmental justice leaders also noted the effects of climate change on farm and construction workers who are increasingly susceptible to respiratory ailments and heat-related problems. Some also discussed how "climate change would affect the cost of doing business in California, and possible impacts on employment due to increased outsourcing [Cordova et al. 2006: 75].

The literature suggests that the impacts of climate change on agriculture, forestry, fishing, and tourism could make communities that depend on those industries vulnerable. Karl et al. (2009) described how the vulnerability of communities is linked to surrounding landscapes by way of agricultural and forestry activities and to somewhat distant landscapes by way of water supplies.

...communities that have developed near areas of agricultural production, such as the Midwest cornbelt or the wine-producing regions of California and the Northwest, depend on the continued productivity of those regions, which would be compromised by increased temperature or severe weather [Karl et al. 2009: 103].

Keller Jensen (2009) described critics of HR 2454 (which would implement a cap-and-trade system to reduce greenhouse gas emissions) who claim it will negatively affect areas that rely on coal for energy and employment and could increase energy costs to a population that might not be able to afford them. Citing concerns raised by Laasby (2009), Keller Jensen cautioned that increased energy costs might move industrial jobs overseas and have a further negative effect on rural areas.

Karl et al. (2009) maintained that areas that depend on tourism-based economies are vulnerable to climate impacts. They described the potential for shifting species ranges and the impacts on hunting and fishing activities, drought and reduced water resources and the impacts on water recreation, and rising temperatures and the impacts on seasons. They cited the examples of expanding seasons for some outdoor activities such as cycling, and reducing seasons for other activities such as skiing.

Proximity to sensitive areas is a concern for coastal communities as well. Coastal communities in Canada are now considered to be vulnerable to climate change, given their location and isolation, exposure to extreme climate variability, and dependence on environmental resources for continued community health and well-being (Dolan and Ommer 2008). Dolan and Ommer (2008) noted the impact of climate change on coastal fisheries and discussed the change in fish patterns with the warming of water, red tide, and other types of algal blooms. They noted that economic losses owing to climate change for socially marginalized people in coastal communities, "including the quantity and quality of plants and marine animals upon which the livelihoods of many coast peoples depends, will have consequences for people's health and well-being" (2008: 30). The authors also discussed the marginalization of some people in coastal communities who are less likely to have the economic resources to effectively respond and adapt to increased stressors.

Jungwirth (2009: 3) showed that the increasing incidence of forest fires in northern California have led to the "decline of our tourism/recreation industry [and] the loss of our precious timber industry," two sectors that have lifted the rural economy and provided jobs for its residents.

Liverman and Merideth (2002) described the role of agriculture in the economy of the Southwest, its impact on water resources in that it covers a relatively small amount of land but consumes 80 percent of water resources, and its vulnerability to localized climate events. They pointed out that many crops are sensitive to droughts, pests, disease, and temperature changes. They mentioned the potential economic vulnerability of agriculture and ranching (which are rain dependent) and forestry (which is sensitive to drought and increased temperatures). Impacts could be severe locally, but minimal if spread out regionally. The effects could be linked to feed prices and external market forces.

Climate change might have a unique effect on Canadian agriculture because warmer temperatures might increase the agricultural output potential (Wall 2008). "Projected increased temperatures could extend growing seasons and allow for production of new varieties in forestry and agriculture," with "extended harvests and the potential for enhanced yields" (Wall 2008: 4).

Davidson et al. (2003) suggested that climate change might increase the timber supply in the United States, which would decrease the need for timber exports from Canada, thus harming the forest-based economy in Canada. They pointed out that tourism in Canadian forests has the potential to increase in the summer with warmer temperatures and decrease in the winter as snow activities are compromised.

Poor populations in rural areas have increased vulnerability because they lack financial resources. Liverman and Merideth (2002) stated that rural populations in the Southwest may be unable to afford higher energy and water costs. They may be unable to afford health or property insurance, and consequently the health care, protections, and repairs needed resulting from climate impacts.

Eriksen et al. (2007: 17) reported that rural economies are often built on farm activities, but "even though non-farm activities are becoming more important, most people are unable to access formal sector income opportunities and instead resort to informal activities both in rural and urban areas which may yield a less secure and/ or smaller income." Although these off-farm activities are increasing in importance, they often do not generate enough income to ensure basic necessities for poor populations. This situation will worsen with climate change.

Rural workforce issues—
Davidson et al. (2003: 2257) showed that residents of resource-dependent communities tend to be less educated and more highly specialized than other residents. Those "highly specialized skills are not easily transferable to other sectors during economic decline or transition."

Rural areas that rely on tourism in addition to natural resources could suffer "from low lake levels, high sea levels, reduced sports fishing, and poor snow conditions" (Wall 2008: 5). However, other outdoor activities, such as golf and camping, could see an increase in use, which might counteract decreases in other activities. Wall (2008: 5) also suggested that "rural Canadian regions, where residents must deal with job and income losses, limited education opportunities, and reduced service levels, have few resources to mobilize when handling a climate-related risk or opportunity."

Wall and Marzall (2006: 376) discussed the state of employment in rural communities, maintaining that there are "limited human capital and highly specialized skill sets that reduce rural residents' ability to move into forms of employment outside resource sectors."

The literature illustrates that rural economies and jobs are increasingly vulnerable as the climate changes. Liverman and Merideth (2002) suggested that the poor who live on tribal lands and in colonias in the Southwest may be the first workers laid off if employers have to make cuts. The state of economies and jobs in rural, resource-based areas is fragile (Wall and Marzall 2006). "If community employment is largely dependent on one resource base, the chances of adapting by moving to another sector are limited" (Wall and Marzall 2006: 385).

Transportation and Urbanization

Issues associated with access to transportation are exacerbated by extreme weather events associated with climate change. Morello-Frosch et al. (2009) raised the concern that a higher proportion of people of color do not have access to a car, which restricts their ability to move to cooler places or government-sponsored cooling stations during extreme heat events. In addition, transportation routes providing vital services, such as the distribution of food, goods, and medical supplies to coastal communities, are vulnerable to storm surges and hurricanes and other extreme weather events (Dolan and Ommer 2008).

Large cities face unique vulnerabilities to climate change because of their expansion, complexity, and interconnectedness with regional and national economies and infrastructure (Karl et al. 2009). With more than 80 percent of the U.S. population residing in urban areas, extreme weather events that affect water and other supplies may be particularly devastating in cities. However, Karl et al. (2009) stated that cities also have the potential to address climate impacts through infrastructure upgrades, efficient transportation, and technology such as hazard warning systems.

Natural Resources

Pandey (2006) identified areas in which the impacts of climate change have already been observed, including agriculture, forestry, fisheries, water, tropical soils, specific plant and animal species, and other natural resources on which rural communities in developing countries rely for their livelihoods. In so doing, Pandey linked rural community vulnerability to the impacts of climate change on natural resources and ecosystem services.

Forests—

Innes (2005) noted that most foresters are educated in the biophysical aspects of forest management, but do not know how to react to the recent shift in forestry to emphasize the role of forests in the communities that live in or near them and use them for their livelihoods. Forest communities with direct influence on forest management will have the power to protect their needs better than those under the control of others (Innes 2005). Innes (2005) listed several risks of climate change on forests and communities that rely on forests. They included plantation failures owing to poor adaptation, extreme climatic events, increased insect or disease problems, increased frequency and severity of fires, unacceptable levels of tree mortality, changes in forest composition, loss of productivity (wood volume), and loss of pulp quality. Davidson et al. (2003) predicted a decline in the range of boreal forest in northern Canada and potential associated effects on forest-based communities.

Karl et al. (2009) described the vulnerability of city water supplies to climate impacts:

> Most cities depend on water supplies from distant watersheds, and those depending on diminishing supplies (such as the Sierra Nevada snowpack) are vulnerable. Northwest communities also depend upon forest resources for their economic base, and many island, coastal, and "sunbelt" communities depend on tourism [Karl et al. 2009: 104].

Keller Jensen (2009) discussed the pine beetle epidemic in the mountain West, citing warmer winters as the main culprit for the loss of more than 7 million acres of forest to beetle infestations. She noted that although some logging companies have been able to benefit from the dead trees, the negative impacts have been significant, especially in areas that had to be closed off owing to fears of forest fires and falling trees.

Floods and extreme weather events—

Changes in precipitation patterns that come with climate change could bring more floods, droughts, and extreme storms that will have significant impacts on agriculture in rural areas (Keller Jensen 2009). Oxfam America (2009) stated that rural communities in the Southeastern United States are particularly vulnerable to climate change-related hazards because of the area's hazard exposures and the growing presence of Latino families who depend on extractive industries, such as fishing, oil, and gas. Oxfam America (2009) pointed out that local government early warning systems for hazards, if they exist, may not reach all Latino families because some may be unable to understand English and others may be undocumented and avoid evacuations because they fear deportation.

Food Security

Warmer water temperatures may lead to increased contaminant uptake by aquatic species including fish (Karl et al. 2009). This poses risks to humans (located in urban or rural areas) who rely on those fish for food.

> In lakes with contaminated sediment, warmer water and low-oxygen conditions can more readily mobilize mercury and other persistent pollutants. In such cases, where these increasing quantities of contaminants are taken up in the aquatic food chain, there will be additional potential for health hazards for species that eat fish from the lakes, including people [Karl et al. 2009: 122].

Land Use and Development

Karl et al. (2009) projected population increases for geographic areas that are particularly vulnerable to climate impacts; thus more Americans could be at risk to climate impacts. They reported that populations are expected to increase considerably in the mountain West and southern coastal areas; populations in California, Texas, Florida, and New York have increased considerably in recent decades. The mountain West is vulnerable to increased wildfires and less available water; the southern coasts are most vulnerable to an increased number of hurricanes, storm surges, and rises in sea level.

> Overlaying projections of future climate change and its impacts on expected changes in U.S. population and development patterns reveals a critical insight: more Americans will be living in the areas that are most vulnerable to the effects of climate change [Karl et al. 2009: 100].

The authors questioned whether communities will implement measures to protect against population growth, development, and associated risks in vulnerable geographic areas. They believed that humans and their land use settlement and development patterns will affect future vulnerability to climate impacts.

Karl et al. (2009) described the vulnerability of the Florida "sunbelt" owing to recent population growth, projected climate impacts, and social factors such as difficulty in finding access to insurance.

> Future population growth and the quality of life for existing residents is likely to be affected by the many challenges associated with climate change, such as reduced insurance availability, increased insurance cost, and increases in water scarcity, sea-level rise, extreme weather events, and heat stress. Some of these problems, such as increasing heat and declining air quality, will be especially acute in cities [Karl et al. 2009: 116].

The report shows that mid-sized towns are growing rapidly in southern parts of the Great Plains region, where available water resources are already constrained and vulnerable urban populations could be disproportionately affected by heat.

American Indian and Alaska Native Tribes

Tribes have unique rights, cultures, and economies that are connected to the land and vulnerable to climate change. Tribes have treaties with the federal government and rights to water and hunting, fishing, and cultural practices that the federal government has the responsibility to protect. A growing body of literature explores the impacts of climate change on indigenous populations in the United States. Because of the amount of available literature on this subject, this section explores both tribal equity issues related to climate change and the specific impacts and challenges faced by American Indian and Alaska Native tribes for a number of different sectors, including public health, employment, and natural resources.

Context

The federal government recognizes 562 tribes in the Lower 48 States and Alaska. Additional tribes exist that are unrecognized by the federal government and ineligible for federal services. Some tribes are recognized only by individual states. In 2000, American Indians and Alaska Natives made up 1.53 percent of the U.S. population, or 4,315,865 people. Full-time, year-round American Indian and Alaska Native workers earned less than average workers in the United States. A greater number of American Indians and Alaska Natives lived in poverty compared to the total U.S. population; one-third of the American Indian and Alaska Native population lived on reservations or in Alaska Native villages. Overall, the population was younger than the total U.S. population (Ogunwole 2006).

In the Lower 48 States, American Indian tribes hold about 3 percent of the land, or 56 million acres; in Alaska, Alaska Native corporations hold about 11 percent, or 44 million acres (Houser et al. 2000). In some states, American Indian tribes hold a small proportion of the land, but they hold a significant proportion in others. In Arizona, for example, tribes hold 27 percent of the land (Liverman and Merideth 2002). With this in mind, we explore why it is important to consider how climate impacts could affect the legal status, cultures, economies, communities, and capacities of American Indian and Alaska Native tribes, and how impacts on tribes could differ from impacts on other populations.

Academic and gray literature suggests that for indigenous peoples, the environmental impacts of climate change and some of the proposed solutions threaten ways of life, subsistence, economic ventures, future growth, cultural survivability, rights, land ownership, and access to resources—natural, cultural, technical, and financial (Nilsson 2008, Tsosie 2007). Because of these risks, American Indian and Alaska Native tribes are expected to suffer the effects of climate change disproportionately compared to nonnative communities (Hanna 2007, Williams and Hardison 2008).

To develop legal and policy approaches useful in protecting the rights of tribes and resources of concern in the face of climate change and climate policy development in the United States, the literature suggests that it is important to understand the social vulnerability of indigenous peoples and their adaptive capacity to address climate change (Wesche and Armitage 2006). Ethics and equity are important considerations for climate change policy and planning to gain an understanding of the vulnerability and the insight of indigenous peoples (Nilsson 2008).

For information specific to indigenous peoples in the United States, a few key reports offered considerations, including Hanna (2007), published through the University of Colorado Law School. This study synthesized and organized in case studies information on climate risks to tribes in Alaska, the Pacific Northwest, the Southwest, and Florida. Houser et al. (2000) focused on climate risks to native peoples and homelands. Additional articles and reports cited these studies in describing climate risks to tribes.

Equity, Justice, and Ethics

The impacts of climate change and proposed solutions threaten the rights of indigenous peoples worldwide. Whole communities are in danger from rising sea levels, increasing numbers and intensity of extreme events, including hurricanes, shifting species ranges, and slow declines in precipitation and available fresh water (Nilsson 2008). Nilsson offered that these impacts come with concerns about rights, land ownership, and access to natural, cultural, technical, and financial resources.

Hanna (2007) discussed climate science based on the Intergovernmental Panel on Climate Change (IPCC) fourth assessment report and how changes in climate affect tribes and their rights in four regions of the United States: the Pacific Northwest, Alaska, the Southwest, and Florida. He also discussed the federal government's legal and fiduciary responsibility regarding climate impacts to tribes and described how climate change will affect American Indian and Alaska Native tribes disproportionately. This is particularly true when one considers their small contributions to the drivers of climate change, the occurring and potential impacts on their cultures, subsistence practices, water rights, and land ownership, and the need for mitigation and adaptation assistance.

Hanna (2007) maintained that climate change threatens the rights of tribes to inhabit lands and continue social and cultural practices on those lands. For Alaska

Native tribes, flooding, erosion, melting, and the loss of traditional knowledge associated with subsistence activities could affect tribal sovereignty. For tribes in Florida, "...climate impacts threaten their basic rights of self-determination because tribal land bases are vulnerable." For example, "rising sea levels pose a grave danger to the Everglades, threatening not only the continuation of the tribal way of life, but the very lands on which it is practiced" (Hanna 2007: 27).

Protecting the rights of tribes—
Williams and Hardison (2005, 2007, 2008) described the impacts of climate change on American Indian and Alaska Native tribes and advocated for federal action to address the occurring and potential effects on tribal homelands, cultures, social practices, and rights. The authors (2008) stated that the impacts of climate change threaten the legal obligation of the United States to protect tribes and the natural and cultural resources, sacred sites, and native homelands on which they depend for physical and spiritual well-being, livelihood, subsistence, and sovereignty. The rights of tribes are connected to specific lands with fixed boundaries, including reservations and federally managed lands that cover traditional territories and traditional-use areas.

> Because of their unique political history, their recognized prior rights and treaty rights only apply to their reservations and usual and accustomed lands. Moving from these lands to adapt to large-scale environmental decline would cut them off from their origins, the places of their collective memory, and the rights to self-determination the Tribes possess as peoples [Williams and Hardison 2005: 10].

In their policy paper to the Obama administration, LaDuke et al. (2009) advocated for recognition of the disproportionate impacts of climate change and energy development on American Indian reservations and Alaska Native villages. Because of the intimate connection between indigenous peoples and the land through culture and subsistence, climate impacts are greatest in Native communities (LaDuke et al. 2009). These authors pushed for the participation of Native communities (often poor with high unemployment rates, lacking adequate housing, and politically isolated) in climate and energy policy. The paper advocates for the opportunity to develop green reservation economies and to stop the exploitation of Native communities and lands. It elaborates that renewable energy and energy efficiency projects could provide Native communities an opportunity to develop their economies and protect their life ways and lands. Federal government leadership and promotion of equitable climate and energy policies are needed to ensure just government-to-government relations and opportunities for native communities.

LaDuke et al. (2009) advocated for the United States to take responsibility for its contributions to climate change and human rights violations, including signing the United Nations Declaration on the Rights of Indigenous Peoples. LaDuke et al. (2009) suggested that the indigenous village of Shishmaref, Alaska, must relocate as a result of rising temperatures, melting ice, and erosion, which could cost taxpayers $180 million. The authors maintained that climate change could force an estimated 180 Alaska villages to relocate at a cost of $1.5 million per household; otherwise these communities will be lost.

Krakoff (2008) (relying on Hanna [2007] and the IPCC report [Parry et al. 2007]) used four cases to examine the physical effects of climate change on American Indian and Alaska Native communities. Rising sea levels, melting sea ice, and thawing permafrost are causing coastal erosion and destroying some Alaska Native villages. She pointed out the potential cultural, religious, and traditional losses associated with relocation. "Due to climate change, Alaska Native communities are facing a cultural loss as profound as that suffered by the Plains tribes when they were confined to reservations and forced to abandon the practices that gave their lives meaning" (Krakoff 2008: 17). Tsosie (2007) considered a climate policy of relocation and suggested that it would inherently continue the injustice and oppression endured by American Indians throughout their relationship with the United States.[2] Parry et al. (2007) stated that relocation for some communities may now be unavoidable.

Tribal treaty rights—

Williams and Hardison (2005) pointed out that the language captured in treaties, the documents that for many tribes serve as a basis for their rights, reflects a belief that the environment exists in a fixed state and resources are inexhaustible. Williams and Hardison (2008) raised questions about the rights of tribes to culturally important species and sites and the cultural sustainability of tribes based on species and lands. They questioned the capacity of tribes as resource-dependent peoples to adapt to climate change based on the level of exposure, sensitivity to impacts, and limited ability to pay the costs associated with addressing climate change.

Cordalis and Suagee (2008) noted that climate changes will add stress to salmon populations in the Pacific Northwest and affect off-reservation fishing rights. Treaty rights to fishing will be of little use if salmon runs no longer occur in Northwest rivers.

---

[2] "The United States' own history of removing Native communities from their traditional lands illustrates the tremendous loss of life and culture that occurs as a result of these policies. It would be a grave injustice to repeat this genocidal past as a supposedly beneficial contemporary policy of 'adaptation' to climate change" (Tsosie 2007: 1646).

The U.S. national assessment of the potential consequences of climate variability and change in the United States (National Assessment Synthesis Team 2000) includes a focus on the potential impacts of climate change on Native peoples and Native homelands in the United States and the Pacific and Caribbean Islands. The authors identified general issues that many American Indians and Alaska Natives face in the context of climate change, but acknowledged that each tribe faces its own local climate change challenges. Houser et al. (2000) showed how climate change impacts on reservation lands and traditional territories or homelands (larger land areas extending beyond the bounds of reservations) will affect American Indians and Alaska Natives. They described the potential impacts of climate change on tribal economies, housing, health, water supplies, livelihood, well-being, sacred sites, and cultural traditions. They considered the tools Native peoples bring to climate change adaptation planning and preparation through culture and experience (Houser et al. 2000).

Houser et al. (2000) discussed the court decision of *Winters v. U.S.* [207 US 564 (1908)], which acknowledged that treaties between the federal government and tribes implicitly reserve for tribes enough water to meet the needs of reservations. Because of this decision, Houser et al. (2000) suggested that, in the context of climate change, the federal government has the responsibility to maintain adequate water supplies for tribes and reservations. The authors noted that under the Winters Doctrine, water rights are quantified, based on the concept of "practicable irrigable acres," providing enough water to meet cultural, domestic, recreational, agricultural, and livestock uses (and in some cases instream flows). They suggested that changes in the amount of available water resources and variation in seasonal timing could affect water allocations as well as water agreements and management.

Hanna (2007) described the federal government's responsibility to protect tribal water rights but pointed out the lack of similar responsibility and incentives for states to do so. He described the McCarran Amendment, which Congress passed in 1952, that allows for state courts to divide the rights to water for a given resource.

[The McCarran Amendment] has allowed states to initiate entire stream basin adjudications, and currently over 60 tribal water cases are pending in state courts. There is some sentiment among tribes that state ability to initiate stream adjudications and determine tribal water rights leads to unfair and inconsistent results for tribes depending on political sentiment, relative strength of legal representation, and state budget allocation. On the other hand, the intensification of water scarcity issues will affect tribal and nontribal interests alike, so the possibility of comprehensive adjudications might become increasingly important to provide all stakeholders with legal certainty regarding their water rights [Hanna 2007: 24].

Karl et al. (2009) maintained that large, unquantified tribal water rights pose challenges to water uses in the West. They noted the already stressed water resources in the Southwest: groundwater pumping lowers water tables, and rising temperatures reduce streamflows. They projected that further climate stresses and population growth will lead to conflicts among water users. Karl et al. (2009) stated that current water agreements in the Southwest over-allocate available water resources (The Colorado River Compact), are disputed (Mexico/U.S. water treaties for the Rio Grande and Colorado Rivers), or are yet to be worked out (Native American water rights).

In considering the climate impacts on water and, in turn, water rights on sovereign tribes in the Southwest, Hanna (2007) stated that quantifying, acquiring, and using water rights are complex processes involving numerous users and legalities. Hanna (2007) described the conflict between the appropriation doctrine governing nontribal water rights and tribal water rights. He highlighted an important consideration regarding the Winters Doctrine and tribal and nontribal water rights in the face of climate change.

It must be noted, though, that despite the unmistakable date of priority assigned to a given tribe pursuant to *Winters*, the scope and tangibility of such rights when not yet put into actual use is quite grey. That is, western water law allows for actual use of water by non-Indians even if tribal legal title or right to use such water is in place; if a tribe later tried to convert its paper right to the water into actual use, the issue is whether that water is thus made unavailable for use by other vested parties. Such tribal assertion of water rights has never yet "shut the gate," so to speak, for other water users, but the impacts resulting from climate change raises the question of how such a situation would be resolved [Hanna 2007: 23].

Liverman and Merideth (2002) also considered the impacts of climate change on water rights and associated impacts on American Indian lands in the Southwest, suggesting the rights to water in the region have been fully allocated among federal agencies, tribal governments, and Mexico, but disputes remain. Liverman and Merideth (2002) suggested that the current unresolved water rights disputes could contribute to the vulnerability of tribes to water declines. They described conflict-ridden cases (The Gila River Adjudication, *Cappaert vs. U.S.* 1976) that could reduce or increase the vulnerability of tribes to water shortages. Compacts, treaties, and unresolved disputes could affect management of water resources and creation of adaptive strategies.

Tribal land ownership and access—

In addition to land loss and legal issues of relocation, the patchwork patterns of land ownership and attached laws that now compose landscapes could affect the ability of tribes to access important lands and resources under changing conditions. Reservations now constrict tribes' access and mobility and could contribute to their vulnerability to climate change, for example as species' ranges shift and they remain with limited options for relocation (Karl et al. 2009). Houser et al. (2000) described the challenges surrounding land use and natural resource management on and around reservations. They considered past management of reservation lands by the federal government, the limited control tribes have had over their lands, coordination of management across land ownership and access, and recognition of the rights of tribes to areas outside of reservations, but within traditional territories. Houser et al. (2000) suggested challenges regarding tribal land ownership and access must be considered in planning for climate change.

As a result of allotment-era polices in the United States, a considerable number of non-Indians live, work, and lease lands on reservations. "Many tribes face severe legal difficulties in creating or enforcing comprehensive plans for land use or natural resource management, a situation that will complicate planning for climate change" (Houser et al. 2000: 356).

Changing conditions could bring into question the ability of existing laws and ownership to uphold rights. "Tribes are tied to their lands through their ancestors, and by legal definition that sets up reservations, outside of which they have limited rights so that they may no longer move and track environmental changes" (Williams and Hardison 2007: 5).

Hansen (2009) described the impacts of climate change on the Quileute, Hoh, Quinault, and Makah Tribes along the west coast of Washington state's Olympic Peninsula. These tribes have coped with extreme weather events for centuries and are now some of the first in the Western United States to face the impacts of climate change. Specifically, Hansen described the occurring and potential effects of coastal erosion, extreme storms, and rising sea levels on tribal land bases, culture, subsistence, and economies.

Climate change threatens existing tribal land bases on the Olympic coast and, to cope, the tribes need access to additional lands within their traditional territories (Hansen 2009). In addition to designated wilderness lands, the area has federal and international designations and residents to consider, including four Indian reservations, nonnative residents, the 135-mile Olympic coastline, a National Marine Sanctuary, Olympic National Park, a United Nations World Heritage Site, International Biosphere Reserve, and designated wilderness area (Hansen 2009). For land to be returned to the tribes, according to Hansen, Congress will need to approve boundary changes for the park and remove the wilderness designation.

The Quileute Indian Tribe's land base (only 1 square mile, bounded by Olympic National Park on three sides and the ocean on the fourth) is most vulnerable to the impacts of climate change. The Quileute Tribe has tried for the past 50 years to negotiate with the Park Service to regain access to additional land to relocate buildings, including the Quileute School, and build housing for the tribe's growing population (Hansen 2009). Hansen described existing disagreements regarding land ownership between the tribe and Park Service and recent attempts to address the conflicts.

Hansen also described the Hoh Tribe's land access and ownership concerns and legal actions to regain land. A local resident highlights how coastal erosion has already washed away homes in past Hoh Tribal village sites and currently threatens a Hoh Tribal cemetery:

> Ward points to the cemetery on an embankment just beyond the abandoned
> village that sits below their present day village. "We buried them in the old
> way, so they could watch the ocean. What's going to happen if the waves
> reach them?" Looters looking for beads and the regalia buried with them
> are a big concern for Ward, especially if the waves uncover them. "We
> have no land to move them to" [Hansen 2009].

In a *Washington Post* article, Lydersen (2009) described the impacts of environmental and land use changes on the wetlands along the southwest coast of Louisiana and the effects of those impacts on Native American tribes—the Houma, Biloxi-Chitimacha-Choctaw, and Pointe-au-Chien Tribes. The article links the impacts of hurricanes and resulting losses of marshes and islands, saltwater intrusion into inland waters and soils (from hurricanes and years of wetland degradation), levees channeling the Mississippi River, and the 10,000 miles (16 090 kilometers) of oil and gas industry canals. The article does not mention "climate change" directly but does describe changes in weather and environment and the resulting impacts on land use, access, economy and jobs, culture, and sense of place.

Lydersen (2009) stated that Louisiana recognizes the Houma, Biloxi-Chitimacha-Choctaw, and Pointe-au-Chien Tribes, but the federal government does not; these tribes fled from persecution to the Louisiana bayous in the early 1800s and now may need to relocate again as hurricane damage and saltwater intrusion inundate and degrade their lands.

Hansen (2009) discussed a National Wildlife Federation report on sea level rise and coastal habitats in the Pacific Northwest to describe how the conflicts between the Hoh, Makah, Quinault, and Quileute Tribes and the National Park Service in Washington state over access to additional land to cope with the environmental impacts of climate change will set a precedent regarding the treatment of vulnerable populations nationwide. Hansen highlighted the report's findings of disproportionate impacts to vulnerable populations, including minorities, poor people, and developing countries; treatment of vulnerable populations will provide a view on how the United States will deal with the impact nationwide.

Self-determination—

Like indigenous peoples worldwide, American Indian and Alaska Native tribes have the right to participate in international decision- and policymaking processes (UN Declaration on the Rights of Indigenous Peoples and Agenda 21). In the United States, tribes have the right to autonomy and self-governance (Indian Self-Determination and Education Assistance Act of 1975). Houser et al. (2000) pointed out that how the rights of tribes are treated in federal policy will affect the abilities of tribes to respond to climate change, from governance to natural resource management.

In an article published in the American Bar Association's *Natural Resources and Environment* publication, Cordalis and Suagee (2008) described how climate change is affecting and will affect Native American and Alaska Native tribes. They suggested it will affect tribes differently than other populations that make up American society. Cordalis and Suagee (2008) considered how tribal governments fit into the "collective human responsibility" to address climate change and questioned the opportunities tribes have to exercise their sovereignty and be involved in federal, state, and local efforts to form and implement climate change policies and programs.

Cordalis and Suagee (2008) noted that tribal sovereignty provides tribal governments the ability to develop and implement their own plans and initiatives to address climate change. However, the role of tribal governments in climate change is currently being overlooked at the federal level. The government in the United States commonly considers federal, state, and local governments, but omits tribal governments (Cordalis and Suagee 2008).

In an editorial published in *Indian Country Today*, Suagee (2009) considered how the American Clean Energy and Security Act (H.R. 2454, also known as Waxman-Markey) could affect American Indians. The author described one of the bill's key features—a cap-and-trade system to reduce greenhouse gas emissions through market forces. The system's guidelines currently outline giving most of the allowances to the electric power industry, giving some to states for energy efficiency and renewable energy programs, and auctioning some to the Environmental

Protection Agency for an energy refund program and climate change adaptation. Suagee suggested the need for national climate legislation to incorporate opportunity for American Indian tribes to address climate change, as it does for states. Suagee (2009) noted that fossil fuel and renewable energy industry representatives, environmental groups, and states have lobbied the Waxman-Markey bill heavily. However, only a small number of tribal representatives have advocated for including provisions for tribes.

Procedural and distributive dimensions of equity—
Suagee (2009) considered the disproportionate distribution of funds under the Waxman-Markey bill and pointed out the difference in opportunity for states and tribal governments to develop energy efficiency, renewable energy, and carbon sequestration efforts, and adapt to climate change under the bill. Under Section 132 of the bill, states would receive allowances for state energy and environment development (SEED) accounts based on a formula that considers population and energy consumption; states would not have to compete for allowances. Section 133, "Support for Indian Renewable Energy and Energy Efficiency Programs," would fund a tribal program with one-half of one percent of the allowances allocated for the SEED accounts. Tribes would compete for allowances under the program.

Gilligan et al. (2006) described the importance of considering and incorporating traditional knowledge along with scientific and local knowledge into climate policies and plans. The authors pointed out the widespread suppression or marginalization of traditional knowledge even though evidence exists to support its value throughout history. Coal and uranium mining and power generation activities provide numerous jobs for Navajo and Hopi peoples, and climate change mitigation policies could affect existing jobs (Smith 2008).

As a result of less ice in Arctic waters, there is potential for increased shipping activity and marine access to increase economic opportunities and affect wildlife habitat and ecosystems through increased land development (Hanna 2007). Greater marine access could bring additional oil industry jobs and revenue to support livelihoods, but at the same time could harm important subsistence resources (Hanna 2007). Lydersen (2009) reported that 10,000 miles (16 090 kilometers) of oil and gas industry canals off the Gulf coast are among the factors affecting the wetlands of southwest Louisiana and, in turn, the life ways of the Houma, Biloxi-Chitimacha-Choctaw, and Pointe-au-Chien Tribes. However, Lydersen pointed out that the industry also provides jobs for tribe members and will continue to do so as wetlands decline and make subsistence and economic shrimping, fishing, farming, hunting, and trapping no longer possible.

Climate justice—

Climate change may exacerbate existing environmental and social stresses and inequities and introduce new issues (Adger 2006). In describing the opportunity for a just climate and energy policy, LaDuke et al. (2009) highlighted the injustice that tribes have endured in the past and continue to endure as a result of energy resource exploitation on tribal lands. They described the impacts of uranium mining, oil extraction, and electricity production on the health, cultures, and rights of tribes.

> Even the most recent federal energy legislation and incentives are still designed to encourage the development of tribal resources by outside corporate interests without ownership or equity participation of the host tribes [LaDuke et al. 2009: 1].

LaDuke et al. (2009) also provided a list of considerations for energy resource development, including the following climate justice concerns.

- Nuclear power is not a just or economically viable solution to climate change, and poses disproportionate impacts on Native communities.
- Oil drilling within the outer continental shelf areas of Alaska poses threats to the life ways and health of Alaska Natives (and continues oil dependence).
- The extraction of carbon-intensive oil from the tar sands in Canada poses threats to the land on which First Nations in Canada rely. It also means reliance on a fuel source many times more carbon-intensive and environmentally damaging than conventional fossil-fuel production.
- Unchecked biofuel production threatens biodiversity and food security. It also contributes to climate change and forest destruction worldwide and thus affects native communities.

Smith (2008) described how mining and energy generation activities (the Four Corners Power Plant and the San Juan Generating Station, the Black Mesa mines, and uranium mining) are changing the climate, desecrating sacred sites, impairing cultural practices and subsistence and livelihood activities, polluting the land and water, forcing relocation without compensation, and impairing the health of Hopi and Navajo peoples. Past, current, and proposed mining and power generation activities make Hopi and Navajo peoples increasingly vulnerable to the impacts of climate change.

Culture and Knowledge

The literature describes how environmental changes that result from climate change threaten subsistence and culturally important natural resources, a sense of place, and cultural traditions for American Indian and Alaska Native tribes. "'If we lose the clam beds, well, that is who we are,' says Larry Ralston, Quinault chief of police. 'The cultural and subsistence significance of this is dramatic'" (Hansen 2009).

Some tribal land bases in Florida are in vulnerable areas, low-lying coastal areas, and wetlands that are highly susceptible to inundation and coastal erosion, and therefore traditional practices and current economies on those lands are also at risk (Hanna 2007). Hanna (2007) maintained that impacts to land will affect subsistence hunting, farming, and fishing and associated traditional and social practices.

Cordalis and Suagee (2008) asserted that the survival of some tribal cultures is at risk because of the connections to ecosystems and specific plant and animal species. With species extinctions, declines, and shifts—in addition to existing stresses—tribes could lose their cultural traditions and in turn their identities (Cordalis and Suagee 2008). The impacts from mining and energy generation are contributing to a changing climate and climate vulnerability for the Navajo and Hopi Nations (Smith 2008). Since 1999, drought and pollution threaten water resources and have led to insufficient water supplies. The impacts on water in turn affect Hopi and Navajo traditional practices, including sheep herding, weaving, gathering medicinal plants, and agriculture. Smith suggested culturally and economically important Churro sheep and medicinal plants are decreasing because water is less available. In describing potential and occurring impacts to tribes in the Southwest, Hanna (2007) also pointed out how impacts to water resources affect cultural traditions in which water is sacred and revered.

In describing potential and occurring impacts on tribes in Alaska, Hanna (2007) suggested that impacts on subsistence life ways will affect culture by disrupting social activities and processes associated with food gathering, such as sharing networks. He suggested that climate change will affect subsistence cultures because of population declines in important species and shifts in species ranges. In addition, he pointed to the increased risk, time, and cost involved in subsistence activities. From these changes, there could be effects on health as the reliance on alternative, imported food sources grows and people become less active and spend less time hunting. The author suggested food costs could also increase with the shift. He suggested that impacts will be highly localized, depending on location and specific subsistence activity.

Cordalis and Suagee (2008) described the climate impacts in Alaska, including changing climate patterns that lead to dangerously thin ice conditions and affect the habitats of polar bears and seals and, in turn, the safety of tribes. The authors described changes in species ranges and impacts on traditional knowledge and the transfer of that knowledge among community members and between generations.

These changes raise questions about the future availability of resources for subsistence cultures—people who hunt, fish, trap, and gather much of their food—which remain vitally important in Alaska Native villages. The value villagers place on the process of harvesting subsistence resources is immeasurable, as these practices are fundamental in establishing a sense of family and community. Climate change is threatening the continued viability of these traditional cultures [Cordalis and Suagee 2008: 47].

Karl et al. (2009) described the reliance of Alaska Native communities on harvesting fish, walruses, seals, whales, sea birds, and other marine species. The report maintained that climate changes are already affecting and are projected to further affect marine and freshwater ecosystems, harming important fisheries for Native communities and food chains.

In his consideration of climate impacts on tribes in the Pacific Northwest, Hanna (2007) focused on risks to salmon and, in turn, cultural, social, economic, and spiritual aspects of Pacific Northwest tribes. He described how commercial overfishing, pollution, deforestation, and urban development have already put stress on salmon populations and how climate change further threatens populations to the point of extinction. Climate changes in temperature, precipitation, the hydrologic cycle, and freshwater and ocean environments will impact salmon at all stages of the life cycle and life processes. Hanna (2007) described the long-standing, integral connection between Pacific Northwest tribes and salmon.

Thus, any harm that befalls the Pacific salmon will necessarily harm those tribes whose identity is inextricably bound to these fish. Reductions in salmon populations hastened by climate change threaten to turn this fundamental legal right to fish—a right that is at the heart of the identities and vitality of Pacific Northwest tribes—into little more than a right to drop their lines and nets into waters devoid of salmon [Hanna 2007: 8].

Traditional ecological knowledge—
Berkes et al. (2000: 1252) defined traditional ecological knowledge as "a cumulative body of knowledge, practice, and belief, evolving by adaptive processes and handed down through generations by cultural transmission, about the relationship of living beings (including humans) with one another and with their environment."

The literature suggests that in the context of climate change, traditional ecological knowledge offers insight into indigenous responses to past changes and broadens the understanding of climate changes now occurring, the impact of changes on indigenous communities, and how to respond to the changes. In their book, *Climate*

Change: Linking Traditional and Scientific Knowledge, Riewe and Oakes (2006) described a new approach to climate change research that combines local and traditional knowledge with expert-based science. The book focuses on communities in the Arctic and stresses how traditional and local knowledge are able to give insight into the human dimensions of climate change.

Briggs (2009) provided insight about the efforts of indigenous communities to address environmental issues, particularly climate change. He drew his information from three participants of "Mother Earth: Confronting the Challenge of Climate Change," a symposium hosted by the Smithsonian's National Museum of the American Indian in late June 2009. Briggs (2009) cited Patricia Cochran, an Inupiat Eskimo, chairwoman of the Inuit Circumpolar Council and former executive director of the Alaska Native Science Commission, who described changes that elders are noticing in the Arctic and the importance of incorporating local observations into climate change research. She also explained the application and evolution of traditional knowledge.

> People tend to think of traditional knowledge as a relic, and they don't really understand that traditional knowledge is dynamic; it is all about knowledge gained and used from one generation to the next. We use knowledge not only from the past but also the present to improve upon what we know. The knowledge I learned from my mother and grandmother isn't what I taught my children [Cochran quoted in Briggs 2009].

Wesche and Armitage (2006) described how traditional knowledge helps to frame and understand past adaptation strategies and the interconnectedness of indigenous communities with the land. The authors suggested that traditional knowledge remains important in social and cultural institutions. These include the networking, sharing, and community cohesion associated with hunting, fishing, and harvesting traditional foods; sharing foods among families; and teaching younger generations about land use and cultural identity. Hotain (2006) explored case studies (including the Elders Forum on Climate Change put on by the Prince Albert Grand Council and the Arctic Climate Impact Assessment) that maintain recognition of indigenous knowledge and have taken different approaches to integrate traditional ecological knowledge with scientific knowledge. Coping with and responding to environmental change requires a long and intimate relationship with the land, which indigenous peoples have. However, Hotain (2006) cautioned that climate changes that are occurring currently and projected for the future pose heightened challenges.

Houser et al. (2000) affirmed that the oral histories and traditional ecological knowledge of native peoples across North America offer insight and are useful for understanding climate changes and impacts on human communities.

> What makes [oral] histories especially valuable is that they often record not only the consequences of these climate fluctuations for peoples and for the environment around them, but also the responses that helped the communities to adjust and survive. Thus, the retelling of these events by tribal elders has created a populace that is relatively well informed about how to adapt to external stresses [Houser et al. 2000: 357].

In addition, Houser et al. (2000) suggested that oral histories reflect and differentiate the impacts of land use changes as well as climate fluctuations. The authors related tribal elders' recollections in the Southwest of lush, grassland-lined river valleys in areas that now support only scant vegetation—most likely the result of overgrazing and drought. The principles that underlie subsistence economies have remained an important part of tribal communities. Those principles include personal relationships, generosity, and diversifying resource reliance (Houser et al. 2000). These concepts could prove valuable in addressing climate change because of their ability to share, distribute, and manage risk.

Houser et al. (2000) cautioned that climate change will limit the application of oral histories for two reasons. First, there is potential for climate changes to become more intense and last longer than past climate fluctuations. Second, the connection between past traditions and a mobile lifestyle that involved moving with the seasons and food and water availability is now limited by land development, confinement of Native peoples on reservations, and loss of access to land. The authors connected this limited mobility with vulnerability to climate change and threats to culture.

> Few contemporary tribes can afford the purchase of large tracts of new land, and federal laws hinder the transfer or expansion of tribal jurisdiction. Tribes therefore see their traditional cultures directly endangered by the magnitude of the projected climate change [Houser et al. 2000: 357].

As a result of climate threats to culturally important species and land features, climate change threatens the survival of many indigenous peoples (Tsosie 2007). The impacts of climate change pose threats to the indicators on which the traditional ecological knowledge of indigenous peoples is based: biodiversity, land features, and culturally important species.

> Climate change has a harmful effect on biological diversity and the related knowledge, innovations and practices of indigenous peoples. Traditional

knowledge is an inseparable part of indigenous culture, social structures, economy, livelihoods, beliefs, traditions, customs, customary law, health and their relationship to the local environment [Nilsson 2008: 13].

Hanna (2007: 21) pointed out how more climate variability and extremes could "undermine traditional knowledge bases and the ability to accurately predict the weather as it relates to growing seasons." Climate change threatens the existence of traditional knowledge; in so doing, it affects safety in hunting, travel, and cultural survival (Hanna 2007).

Local knowledge—
The literature also considers the role of local ecological knowledge in understanding climate vulnerability and adaptive capacity. Incorporating local knowledge, the literature suggests, could help engage and benefit local people and complement understanding gained through other knowledge systems (Gilligan et al. 2006, Mallory et al. 2006). Mallory et al. (2006) suggested that local ecological knowledge, in contrast to traditional ecological knowledge, incorporates recent environmental interactions, technology, and other influencing factors. Whereas indigenous peoples hold traditional knowledge, Gilligan et al. (2006) observed that local knowledge can be held by any group of people with environmental and social experiences in common.

Mallory et al. (2006) considered the use of local ecological knowledge as a data source for monitoring wildlife populations in the Western Hudson Bay area of Canada. They stated that local ecological knowledge should be used, but requires a thoughtful approach that recognizes differences between local ecological knowledge and scientific knowledge. Based on a review of research studies that incorporate local ecological knowledge, the study recommends that the best approach would combine it with scientific knowledge. The study describes differences that result from using local ecological knowledge that incorporates recent environmental interactions and traditional ecological knowledge. It considers that technology and other current influencing factors may also add variety to local knowledge not contained in traditional knowledge. According to Mallory et al. (2006), studies that involve local knowledge help engage local people, and local knowledge is best used to complement scientific knowledge in establishing population baselines and leads to more fruitful results.

Multiple knowledge systems—
Brook et al. (2006) considered how to appropriately collect knowledge held by local people that is usually not documented. They considered how to do so without taking it out of its local context and describing it in scientific terms. The authors suggested

that research on traditional ecological knowledge be done "primarily within, and by persons with respect for, understanding of [Inuit] language, culture and customs" (Assembly of First Nations and the Inuit Circumpolar Conference 1994).

Brook et al. (2006) maintained that communities should be involved in all aspects of research studies related to their knowledge, particularly in deciding how to link their local or traditional knowledge with expert-based science, if at all. They noted that local people provide an important perspective on how their knowledge differs from expert-based knowledge. Studies are opportunities for individuals and whole communities to be co-authors on papers, but these papers should explain the nature of the collaboration and how accountability was achieved. Brook et al. (2006) cited researchers who question the validity of integrating traditional knowledge into scientific research and even question its existence. They emphasized the challenges of local knowledge research, particularly when local knowledge and scientific knowledge conflict, and highlighted the need to address and balance power.

> [Assessing local knowledge for quality and validity] represents a value-judgment by researchers and similarly places the balance of power with scientists and managers. This loss of control is particularly evident in many studies where communities have little or no input into study design, study participants are interviewed on a one-time basis and the community receives no further information regarding the study results or opportunity to comment on them [Brook et al. 2006: 15].

Gilligan et al. (2006) described how incorporating different knowledge systems requires a cross-discipline, cross-cultural approach. They emphasized the need to have consent when incorporating or otherwise using information from other knowledge systems, and to do so appropriately and with respect. They stressed the need to have an even, balanced, power structure in research, motivation, methods, and the use of knowledge.

> Once collected, the control over the knowledge becomes that of the researcher, which, in some cases, because of their cultural limitations in understanding a foreign knowledge system, results in the dissection and misinterpretation of the TK [traditional knowledge] and/or LK [local knowledge] [Gilligan et al. 2006: 8].

They cautioned that integrating traditional knowledge with scientific knowledge can fragment the knowledge and take it out of its cultural and social context.

Adaptive Capacity

Coping and response strategies—

In a *News from Indian Country* article, Bryan (2009) described the efforts of Zia Pueblo residents, volunteers, and an ecologist from Santa Fe to restore a spring sacred to the Zia Pueblo tribe. Zia tribe members have made pilgrimages to the spring for generations during the summer solstice to draw water and carry it back to the tribe's village at the base of the Jemez Mountains. The article reports how the group worked to plant native grass seeds and build rock dams above the spring to collect water and sediment coming from the sandstone bluffs and clay hills around the spring. Bryan (2009) highlighted concerns about available water and other natural resources for future generations for Zia Pueblo. In preparing for climate change, Houser et al. (2000) suggested the application of traditional water storage manage-ment practices, similar to those used by the tribes of the Southwest, including Pueblo peoples hundreds of years ago.

Briggs (2009) included Robert Gough's description of the long-term experience of native communities to build energy-efficient homes and adapt to climate changes and natural hazards and stated a desire to see every native community become energy self-sufficient.

In a *SolveClimate News* article, Shin (2009) described the Navajo Nation's recently adopted green jobs legislation and the economic opportunities it promotes, including renewable energy development, organic farming and livestock, and weavers' cooperatives. He described how this legislation could serve as a model for tribes around the world and how the legislation will help to counter coal produc-tion and mining on the reservation. This article does not mention climate change directly but highlights the legislation's potential to develop a tribal economy in line with Navajo culture and traditions and, in the process, reduce the tribe's 44-percent unemployment rate. The article describes the legislation's intent to reduce green-house gas emissions and the impacts of greenhouse gases.

> The Navajo Nation became the first Native American tribe to pass green jobs legislation intended to grow thousands of jobs in ways that follow the Navajo traditions of respecting the earth. The Navajo Nation Council voted to establish a Navajo Green Economy Commission that will draw on federal, state and foundation funding to pay for green initiatives ranging from farmers' markets to small-scale energy projects [Shin 2009].

Hanna (2007) also described legal and policy approaches that tribes are tak-ing and can take now to act on climate change, as the country waits for a federal climate policy. He described general and region-specific approaches for tribes, acknowledging differences in regional impacts and tribal histories and cultures.

- **Protecting cultural identities:** Tribes will need to act to protect cultural identities from climate impacts.

- **Intertribal initiatives:** Intertribal strategies include mitigation planning and renewable energy development, energy-efficient land-use plans and building codes, and carbon sequestration and carbon offset portfolio development. Intertribal strategies also include the need for cooperative intertribal and intergovernmental initiatives to pool resources and build a collective voice for advocacy. Examples of these types of organizations include the Northwest Indian Fisheries Commission and the Columbia River Inter-Tribal Fish Commission.

- **Litigation to motivate governments to act:** Litigation could help motivate governments to mitigate climate change and address the climate costs to society. A number of considerations for tribes regarding litigation include finding issues appropriate for judicial decision, addressing standing to bring a court claim, and practical difficulties, such as cost, resources, and time. Tribal sovereignty might help establish standing.

- **Participation at state, local, and regional levels:** Tribes might consider participation in regional initiatives to address climate change, such as carbon markets and state and local initiatives, such as greenhouse gas mitigation plans.

- **Action at the regional level:** There are numerous legal and policy approaches specific for tribes in the Southwest, Pacific Northwest, Florida, and Alaska to consider as avenues for protecting their rights in the face of climate change. Protections for salmon and water in the Northwest, water rights in the Southwest, human rights and subsistence practices in Alaska, and subsistence, land, and protection against flooding in Florida.

Sectors Affected by Climate Change

Water—

The literature suggests that changes in water availability and timing will affect tribal economies, cultural and social activities, culturally important species, governance, and rights.

Collins (2008) summarized the anticipated content of the International Expert Meeting on Climate Change and Indigenous Peoples held in Darwin, Australia, April 2–4, 2008. The United Nations University's Japan-based Institute of Advanced Studies, the UN Permanent Forum on Indigenous Issues, and the North Australia

Indigenous Land and Sea Management Alliance co-organized the meeting. Its focus was the occurring and projected impacts of climate change on indigenous peoples and the effects of proposed climate mitigation activities. Collins (2008) suggested that impacts from climate-induced drought and reduced water resources will affect governance, access, and rights. They could threaten tribal, resource-based industries and agriculture on leased lands, which could reduce tribal income and, in turn, affect tribal services. He stated that potential decreases in water quantity and quality, rising temperatures, and increased heat waves and wildfires could affect groundwater resources and lead to increased evaporation. In turn, this could affect native plant and wildlife populations, biodiversity, and culturally important species.

Houser et al. (2000) also described how changes in precipitation and water resource availability could affect tribal water rights, culture, and economic activities. Tribes rely on water for spiritual, environmental, and physical health, as well as food production and fish, wildlife, and plant populations. Water is a physical and cultural necessity for tribes, and water is most sacred where it is most scarce, in the Southwest United States (Houser et al. 2000). The combination of past and current land uses, development, and climate change threaten water resources in the Southwest.

Hanna (2007) maintained that the climate impacts to tribes of the Southwest are largely related to water. He described a number of concerns, including the nature of the region's watersheds; existing low flows and high water demand; increases in development, population, and water demand; and the region's rigid legal framework for water allocation. Cordalis and Suagee (2008) also pointed out that climate change will add stress in the Southwest to already diminished and conflict-ridden water sources, which are projected to decline further. The authors note that tribes in New Mexico, Colorado, Utah, Nevada, and California have established water rights within the Colorado River watershed, which will be affected by declines owing to reduced streamflow and snowpack.

Karl et al. (2009) noted the vulnerability of Native communities in the Southwest to reduced water quality and quantity, and presented a map of places where water conflicts are projected to occur by 2025 that delineates Indian lands, Native entities, and rural areas with unmet water needs, and provides ratings of conflict potential of moderate, substantial, and highly likely.

Hanna (2007) stated that for tribes in Florida, saltwater intrusion could affect water resources that supply municipal, agricultural, and commercial activities. For the 65 Native American tribes in the Great Plains region, Karl et al. (2009) suggested that existing water quantity and quality problems on many reservations may reduce the capacity of tribes to respond to climate change.

Public health—

The literature on public health describes how increases in exposure to extreme events, chronic conditions, and lack of access to health services contribute to tribes' vulnerability to the health risks of climate change. Increases in wildfire smoke and dust, for example, could increase respiratory-related health impacts and thus increase the need for health services, which have already been declining in rural areas of the United States owing to declining populations and economies. Houser et al. (2000) noted that increases in reservation populations and the incidence of medical conditions requiring ongoing care, such as diabetes treatment and kidney dialysis, combined with difficulty in accessing health care services, affect Native peoples' health and contribute to their vulnerability to the health risks of climate impacts. LaDuke et al. (2009) also found that reservations nationwide are more vulnerable to climate-related health risks and mortality, including cold, heat, and drought.

Hanna (2007) described the threats of human exposure to contaminants that accumulate through the food chain and are acquired through subsistence practices for Alaska Native tribes. These contaminants are transported by the wind from further south in Canada and the United States. Hanna suggested that these contaminants could lead to immunodeficiency and neurodevelopment problems, but noted that this process is not well understood. He also described the potential for pest and disease outbreaks to lead to increased pesticide use and, in turn, increased exposure of traditional foods and humans to pesticides. Increased shipping activity as a result of less ice in Arctic waters can also raise the potential for hazardous waste spills and, in turn, affect human health (Hanna 2007).

Potential health effects are also projected to affect Florida tribes, including greater susceptibility to heat- and air-quality-related health problems such as heat stroke, as well as vector-borne diseases, which could have greater opportunities for survival and dispersal under warmer water and air temperatures (Hanna 2007). Liverman and Merideth (2002) noted that a large proportion of the people living in poverty in the Southwest are vulnerable to vector-borne disease increases, water shortages, and temperature extremes; they live on tribal lands, in colonias, or in other areas that lack adequate services and have limited access to sanitation and safe drinking water.

Housing—

Native housing is more vulnerable to climate change than the national average because of lower levels of economic development (Houser et al. 2000). As a result, Native peoples have less protection from changing environmental conditions and may have less ability to access solutions, including air conditioners. Adjusting to hotter temperatures would require behavioral shifts to a more indoor lifestyle, improved housing conditions, and electricity, but "a recent study of energy consumption on Indian lands found that reservation households are ten times more likely to be without electricity (14.2 percent) than the national average (1.4 percent)" [Houser et al. 2000: 361].

LaDuke et al. (2009) suggested that reservations have great housing needs. Currently one-third of reservation homes are trailers, which, for the most part, lack weatherization. Reservations are in need of (and waiting for) more than 200,000 new homes. Inadequate housing increases exposure to extreme weather events and vulnerability to financial burdens that result from energy price volatility and weather damage.

Energy—
Literature, including LaDuke et al.'s (2009) letter to the Obama administration, suggests that tribal lands offer renewable energy potential and human resources. LaDuke et al. (2009) proposed that the United States could benefit from involving tribes in climate policy because of the renewable energy resources found on tribal lands.

> A green, carbon-reduced energy policy has major national and international human rights, environmental and financial consequences, and we believe that this administration can provide groundbreaking leadership on this policy. The reality is that the most efficient, green economy will need the vast wind and solar resources that lie on Native American lands. This provides the foundation of not only a green low carbon economy but also catalyzes development of tremendous human and economic potential in the poorest community in the U.S.—Native America [LaDuke et al. 2009: 1].

La Duke et al. (2009) provided statistics showing the potential contributions of reservations to a green economy and renewable energy production. They estimated a wind energy potential on tribal lands of 535 billion kilowatt hours/year and a solar electricity potential of 17,000 billion kilowatt hours/year. The authors maintained that renewable energy investment creates more jobs per dollar invested than does fossil fuel energy and that investment in energy efficiency creates 21.5 jobs for every million dollars invested. Yet, the authors warned that systems for energy transmission on Indian reservations currently are highly vulnerable to power outages during winter storms.

Natural hazards and disasters—

Natural hazards, including blizzards, ice storms, and floods, and resulting electric power outages, transportation problems, fuel depletion, and food supply shortages could isolate tribes (Collins 2008).

Considering Alaska Native tribes and citing a General Accounting Office publication, "Alaska Native Villages: Most Are Affected by Flooding and Erosion, but Few Qualify for Federal Assistance," GAO-04-142 (Dec. 2003), Cordalis and Suagee (2008) stated that to varying extents, erosion and flooding are affecting 86 percent of Alaska Native villages, with the greatest effects being felt along the coast. They described climate change effects in the Inupiaq village of Shismaref, which faces complete destruction from storm surges because the sea ice that diffused storms now melts. The authors noted other Alaska Native villages—Kivalina, Koyukuk, and Newtok—are also at risk, and no funding source is known to exist for assistance. Hanna (2007) also described the damage potential from flooding and erosion, including the need for relocation—already a reality for several Native villages, including Kivalina, Koyukuk, Newtok, and Shismaref. He described the current and potential flooding and erosion damage and the federal and state programs from which assistance could come. He noted that few tribes have benefitted from some of the programs because of the cost-benefit requirements.

Referencing climate scientist Patty Glick, author of a recently published National Wildlife Federation report, "Sea Level Rise and Coastal Habitats in the Pacific Northwest," Hansen (2009) suggested that tectonic rise makes it difficult to know how sea level rise will affect the Olympic coast. However, wave action and force, storm surges, and hurricanes are expected to increase in decades to come, and research indicates a range of possibilities regarding sea level rise. Tsunamis also concern residents, many of whom position their cars, when parking them, in preparation for a quick getaway (Hansen 2009).

In the Southeast, the impacts of hurricanes and saltwater intrusion threaten tribal subsistence and livelihood activities, such as shrimping and collecting oysters; hunting and trapping mink, raccoons, muskrat and nutria; and farming and raising livestock (Lydersen 2009).

In the Southwest, climate impacts could destabilize dune ecosystems and, in turn, diminish habitats for native plants and livestock grazing—which relies primarily on dune vegetation—and damage homes and transportation via blowing sand (Cordalis and Suagee 2008). The authors suggested that the destabilization of dunes could be an indicator of climate change because it results from changes in precipitation, soil moisture, and wind patterns.

Tribal Economies and Jobs

The literature describes how high unemployment rates on reservations currently contribute to the vulnerability of tribal economies in the face of climate change. It considers how climate impacts pose risks to natural resource-based economic activities and traditional and subsistence market-based activities. LaDuke et al. (2009) noted that the unemployment rate on Indian reservations is twice the U.S. national average as is the poverty rate for Native Americans. The growing population of individuals on reservations 18 years of age or older increases demand for adequate housing and jobs.

Changes in temperature and precipitation, increases in extreme weather events, and pest and disease outbreaks will affect tribal nations with economies that depend on tourism, agriculture, and other natural-resource-based industries. They could force transitioning to new activities or adjusting current activities, such as cultural traditions dependent on plant and animal species and specific seasonal conditions that draw tourists to reservations (Houser et al. 2000). Houser et al. (2000) described the importance of natural-resource-based activities for Native peoples' economic development even though they seldom fully meet economic needs. These include dry-land and irrigated agriculture in the West and central United States; forestry in the West, central United States, and Alaska; and tourism and recreation in the West, Southwest, central United States, Hawaii, and Alaska. Many reservation economies and tribal governments depend on revenue from agriculture, forestry, and tourism (Collins 2008).

Cordalis and Suagee (2008) stated that climate change impacts will affect many sectors of tribal economies in the Southwest: agriculture, industry, community development, and tourist-oriented development. Hanna (2007) stated that changes in seasonal timing and flow could affect tourist-based activities and recreation, gaming, and service economies for tribes of the Southwest—particularly water-based recreation but also gaming and the service industry. He described the potential for climate change to positively and negatively impact tourism by extending or decreasing weather and seasons for recreation. Hanna (2007) described the dependence of several Southwest tribes on agricultural economies and the vulnerability of these tribes that lack diversity in their economies because of the potential for climate change to adversely affect agriculture.

Additionally, Hanna (2007) considered impacts on Southeastern tribal economies. The traditional and current economies of Florida's tribes combine agriculture—citrus and sugarcane—and ranching, hunting, trading, gaming, and tourism. These activities are all sensitive to projected climate changes, including rising sea levels and associated impacts to barrier islands that buffer storm surges, estuarine habitats, and groundwater aquifers as freshwater mixes with saltwater. In addition to rising sea levels, rising sea temperatures could kill coral reefs and, as a result, disrupt the entire ocean food chain, including commercial and recreational fishing and diving (Hanna 2007).

Conclusion: Areas for Future Research

This literature synthesis illustrates the growing body of knowledge related to climate change and social vulnerability in the United States. And yet, there is a need for continued research on specific aspects of social vulnerability, as well as strategies for policies and programs in the United States to reflect the lessons learned from this research and the needs of socially vulnerable populations in this country.

Underlying many of the findings and recommendations presented by the authors noted in this synthesis, are knowledge and information gaps that reflect the complexity of the topic. In this conclusion, we acknowledge some of these knowledge gaps as a way to build direction for further research. However, this is not an exhaustive list of research needs pertaining to the social dimensions of climate change.

Issues of climate vulnerability, equity, and justice are fundamentally about accountability for the causes of climate change and responsibility for helping communities and vulnerable populations prepare for the effects. Climate change decisionmaking processes that do not consider climate vulnerability, equity, and justice may fail to adequately provide services, information, education, and support to key segments of society. Social science can assist by framing questions and designing research to clarify disproportional effects of climate change and inequities associated with access to climate information and processes.

This literature synthesis underscores the importance of considering how human populations differ in their response to, and engagement in, climate change processes. Social science that reflects inequities and differences among human populations can be used to inform or modify assumptions made in modeling and assessment about the social dimensions of climate change. Research in the areas of culture, traditional knowledge, sense of place, and rights, including treaty rights for American Indian tribes, will contribute to understanding of how human populations differ in their responses to climate change. New information about the social dimensions of climate change may help improve the relevance and effectiveness of climate change programs and policies.

The literature also reveals that coping and response capacity of human populations is an important dimension of climate vulnerability. A better understanding of adaptive capacity—what makes some populations better equipped to deal with change and take advantage of opportunities to improve how they respond to climate change effects—is needed to inform how local, regional, and national governments and organizations can assist communities in planning for climate change. Similarly, social science can contribute to improved understanding of rural-urban interdependencies, particularly with respect to natural resource management. Research that takes into account multiple scales of governance or land ownerships may be particularly useful in understanding adaptive capacity and rural-urban relationships.

The ways in which access to information, education, and technology contribute to climate change adaptation and mitigation planning are not yet well understood, though often deemed important. Social science research examining access to and participation in climate change policy development and implementation will inform policy and decisionmaking processes while increasing understanding about climate equity and justice. This area of research dovetails with a broader research agenda on the role of race, ethnicity, and gender related to climate change. For example, the literature exploring climate change and American Indian tribes and Alaska Native communities suggests the need for additional understanding about treaty rights and access to on- and off-reservation resources in the context of climate change.

Also, a sizeable literature exists on gender and climate change at the international level, suggesting a need and opportunity to expand research related to gender and climate change in the United States. International research and policy literature on climate change can inform policy, research, and practice here in the United States. Rural, forest-based communities would be a logical population to examine for gender-related impacts of climate change, building on gender-related research previously conducted in those areas on employment and socioeconomic well-being.

In the time since we began this literature synthesis in 2009, there has been a proliferation of new research and publications on topics related to climate change and social vulnerability. Continued exploration of climate change and social vulnerability through social science research will provide the research community and on-the-ground practitioners with a stronger understanding of the populations most at risk. As a result, there will be a stronger understanding of the processes that will be most effective in engaging socially vulnerable populations in reducing greenhouse gas emissions and preparing for the physical effects of climate change.

References

Adger, W.N. 2006. Vulnerability. Global Environmental Change. 16(3): 168–182.

Agrawal, A. 2008. The role of local institutions in adaptation to climate change. Ann Arbor, MI: International Forestry Research and Institutions Program. 47: 3–28.

Ash, M.; Boyce, J.K.; Chang, G.; Pastor, M.; Scoggins, J.; Tran, J. 2009. Justice in the air: tracking toxic pollution from America's industries and companies to our states, cities, and neighborhoods. http://college.usc.edu/pere/documents/justice_in_the_air_web.pdf. (November 2010).

Assembly of First Nations and the Inuit Circumpolar Conference, 1994. A Preliminary Research Prospectus. In: Sadler, B.; and Boothroyd, P., eds, Traditional Ecological Knowledge and Modern Environmental Assessment. Vancouver, BC: University of British Columbia, Centre for Human Settlements: 61–67.

Barber, V. [In preparation]. Social vulnerability and equity in the context of climate change: considerations for socially vulnerable communities in Alaska and Canada. Synthesis of literature. On file with: Valerie Barber, University of Alaska Fairbanks, 533 E Fireweed Ave. Palmer, AK 99645.

Basu, R.; Ostro, B. 2009. A multi-county analysis identifying the vulnerable populations for mortality associated with high ambient temperature in California. Oakland, CA: California Climate Change Center: 9–17.

Bendixen and Associates 2008. National survey of Hispanic voters on environmental issues. http://www.sierraclub.org/ecocentro/survey/analysis.pdf. (November 2010).

Berkes, F.; Colding, J.; Folke, C. 2000. Rediscovery of traditional ecological knowledge as adaptive management. Ecological Applications. 10(5): 1251–1262.

Blakney, S. 2006. Hunting caribou: Inuit adaptation to the land. In: Riewe, R.R.; Oakes, J.E., eds. Climate change: linking traditional and scientific knowledge. Winnipeg, Manitoba: Aboriginal Issues Press: 77–79.

Briggs, K. 2009. Environment: climate change symposium illuminates Native values, approaches. American Indian News Service. http://www.americanindian-news.org/2009/07/ennvironment-climate-climate-symposium-illuminates-native-values-approaches/. (July 12, 2009).

Brook, R.; M'Lot, M.; McLachlan, S. 2006. Pitfalls to avoid when linking traditional and scientific knowledge. In: Riewe, R.R.; Oakes, J.E., eds. Climate change: linking traditional and scientific knowledge. Winnipeg, Manitoba: Aboriginal Issues Press: 13–20.

Brown, K.; Corbera, E. 2003. Exploring equity and sustainable development in the new carbon economy. Climate Policy. 3(S1): 41–56.

Bryan, S.M. 2009. New Mexico tribe works to restore sacred spring. News from Indian Country. http://indiancountrynews.net/index.php?option=com_content&task=view&id=6614&Itemid=5. (June 2009).

Burton, I.; Huq, S.; Lim, B.; Pilifosova, O.; Schipper, E.L. 2002. From impacts assessment to adaptation priorities: the shaping of adaptation policy. Climate Policy. 2(2-3): 145–159.

California Climate Change Public Health Impacts Assessment and Response Collaborative. 2007. Public health impacts of climate change in California: community vulnerability assessments and adaptation strategies. Richmond, CA: California Department of Public Health: 1–49.

Cannon, T. 2000. Vulnerability analysis in disasters. In: Parker, D., ed. Floods. London: Routledge: 43–55.

Clausen, E.; McNeilly, L. 1998. Equity and global climate change: the complex elements of global fairness. Arlington, VA: Pew Center on Global Climate Change: 1–39.

Collins, T. 2008. Indigenous peoples hardest hit by climate change describe impacts: biofuel production, renewable energy expansion, other mitigation measures uprooting indigenous peoples in many regions. International expert meeting on climate change and indigenous peoples. Darwin, Australia: United Nations University. http://www.eurekalert.org/pub_releases/2008-04/unu-iph040108.php. (April 2009).

Cordalis, D.; Suagee, D.B. 2008. The effects of climate change on American Indian and Alaska Native tribes. Natural Resources and Environment. American Bar Association. 22(3): 45–49.

Cordova, R.; Gelobter, M.; Hoerner, A.; Love, J.; Miller, A.; Saenger, C.; Zaidi, D. 2006. Climate change in California: health, economic, and equity impacts. Oakland, CA: Redefining Progress: 11–109

Crump, J. 2008. Many strong voices—climate change and equity in the Arctic and Small Island Developing States. Indigenous Affairs. 1(2): 24–34.

Cutter, S.L.; Finch, C. 2008. Temporal and spatial changes in social vulnerability to natural hazards. Proceedings of the National Academy of Sciences of the United States of America. 105(7): 2301–2307.

Davidson, D.; Williamson, T.; Parkins, J. 2003. Understanding climate change risk and vulnerability in northern forest-based communities. Canadian Journal of Forestry Research. 33: 2252–2261.

Dolan, A.H.; Ommer, R. 2008. Climate change and community health: lessons from Canada's east and west coasts. Journal of Rural and Community Development. 3(2): 27–46.

Environmental Justice and Climate Change Initiative. 2009. What is climate justice? http://www.ejcc.org/cj/. (March 24, 2009).

Eriksen, S.; Klein, R.; Ulsrud, K.; Naess, L.O.; O'Brien, K. 2007. Climate change adaptation and poverty reduction: key interactions and critical measures. Oslo, Norway: Norwegian Agency for Development Cooperation: 4–43.

Few, R. 2006. Health and climatic hazards: framing social research on vulnerability, response and adaptation. Global Environmental Change. 17(2): 281–296.

Ford, J.D.; Smit, B.; Wandel, J.; MacDonald, J. 2006. Vulnerability to climate change in Igloolik, Nunavut: what we can learn from the past and present. Polar Record. 42(221): 127–138.

Fothergill, A.; Peek, L. 2004. Poverty and disasters in the United States: a review of recent sociological findings. Natural Hazards. 32(1): 89–110.

Gamble, J.L.; Ebi, K.L.; Sussman, F.G.; Wilbanks, T.J. 2008. Analyses of the effects of global change on human health and welfare and human systems. A Report by the U.S. Climate Change Science Program and the Subcommittee on Global Change Research. Washington, DC: U.S. Environmental Protection Agency.

Gilligan, J.; Clifford-Pena, J.; Edye-Rowntree, J.; Johansson, K.; Gislason, R.; Green, T.; Arnold, G.; Heath, J.; Brook, R. 2006. The value of integrating traditional, local and scientific knowledge. In: Riewe, R.R.; Oakes, J.E., eds. Climate change: linking traditional and scientific knowledge. Winnipeg, Manitoba: Aboriginal Issues Press: 3–12.

Hanna, J.M. 2007. Native communities and climate change: legal and policy approaches to protect tribal legal rights. Boulder, CO: University of Colorado School of Law: 4–69.

Hansen, T. 2009. NW coastal nations at risk of climate change disruptions. News from Indian Country. April 27. http://indiancountrynews.net/index. php?option=com_content&task=view&id=3080&Itemid=5. (July 24, 2009).

Hoerner, A.J.; Robinson, N. 2008. A climate of change: African Americans, global warming, and a just climate policy for the U.S. Oakland, CA: Environmental Justice and Climate Change Initiative: 7–65.

Hotain, M. 2006. "Ethical space" for indigenous environmental knowledge in policy development. In: Riewe, R.R.; Oakes, J.E., eds. Climate change: linking traditional and scientific knowledge. Winnipeg, Manitoba: Aboriginal Issues Press: 29–35.

Houser, S.; Teller, V.; MacCracken, M.; Gough, R.; Spears, P. 2000. Potential consequences on climate variability and change for Native peoples and homelands. In: U.S. National Assessment Synthesis Team, eds. Climate change impacts in the United States: the potential consequences of climate variability and change. Washington, DC: U.S. Global Change Research Program. http:// www.globalchange.gov/publications/reports/scientific-assessments/first-national-assessment/478. (July 2010).

Ikeme, J. 2003. Equity, environmental justice and sustainability: incomplete approaches in climate change politics. Global Environmental Change. 13(3): 195–206.

Innes, J. 2005. The importance of climate change in considering the role of forests in the alleviation of poverty. Paper presented at 17th Commonwealth forestry conference, Colombo, Sri Lanka. www.cfc2010.org/2005/CFC%20pdfs/J%20 Innes%20paper.pdf. (July 23, 2009).

Jungwirth, L. 2009. The role of federal lands in combating climate change. Testimony to the Subcommittee on National Parks, Forests, and Public Lands of the Committee on Natural Resources. March 3. On file with: Lynn Jungwirth, Watershed Research and Training Center, P.O. Box 356 Hayfork, CA 96041.

Karl, T.R.; Melillo, J.M.; Peterson, T.C., eds. 2009. Global climate change impacts in the United States. Cambridge, United Kingdom: Cambridge University Press. 196 p.

Keating, M. 2004. Air of injustice: how air pollution affects the health of Hispanics and Latinos. Bassford, M.; Ledford, A.; Lemus, G.D., eds. http://www.lulac. org/assets/pdfs/pollutionreport2.pdf. (December 11, 2009).

Keller Jensen, J. 2009. Climate change and rural communities in the U.S. Columbia, MO: Rural Policy Research Institute. www.rupri.org/Forms/ Climate_Change_Brief.pdf. (October 1, 2009).

Krakoff, S. 2008. American Indians, climate change, and ethics for a warming world. Denver, CO: University of Colorado: 1–34.

Laasby, Gitte. 2009. Indiana reps vote no on climate change bill. Post-Tribune, Indiana, June 30, 2009.

LaDuke, W.; Gough, B.; Goldtooth, T. 2009. Energy justice in Native America: a policy paper for consideration by the Obama administration and the 111th Congress. Honor the Earth, Intertribal Council on Utility Policy, Indigenous Environmental Network, and International Indian Treaty Council. www. treatycouncil.org/PDFs/EJ%20in%20NA%20Policy%20Paper.pdf. (July 24, 2009).

LegCo Secretariat. 2005. Definitions of poverty. Subcommittee to Study the Subject of Combating Poverty: FS10/04-05. Research and Library Services Division of LegCo Secretariat, Hong Kong. http://www.legco.gov.hk/yr04-05/ english/sec/library/0405fs10e.pdf. (May 4, 2009).

Liverman, D.M.; Merideth, R. 2002. Climate and society in the U.S. Southwest: the context for a regional assessment. Climate Research. 21: 199–218.

Locatelli, B.; Kanninen, M.; Brockhaus, M.; Pierce Colfer, C.J.; Murdiyarso, D.; Santoso, H. 2008. Facing an uncertain future: how forests and people can adapt to climate change. Bogor, Indonesia: Center for International Forestry Research: 1–100.

Lydersen, K. 2009. Gulf waters imperil tribes' way of life in Louisiana bayous: as wetlands shrink, oil and gas jobs replace farming, fishing and trapping. The Washington Post. July 20. http://www.washingtonpost.com/wp-dyn/content/ article/2009/07/19/AR2009071901819.html?hpid=moreheadlines. (August 2009).

Macchi, M.; Oviedo, G.; Gotheil, S.; Cross, K.; Boedhihartono, A.; Wolfangel, C.; Howell, M. 2008. Indigenous and traditional peoples and climate change. Gland, Switzerland: International Union for Conservation of Nature: 1–66.

Mallory, M.; Gilchrist, G.; Akearok, J. 2006. Can we establish baseline local ecological knowledge on wildlife populations? In: Riewe, R.R.; Oakes, J.E., eds. Climate change: linking traditional and scientific knowledge. Winnipeg, Manitoba: Aboriginal Issues Press: 21–29.

Morello-Frosch, R.; Pastor, M.; Sadd, J.; Shonkoff, S. 2009. The climate gap: inequalities in how climate change hurts Americans & how to close the gap. Los Angeles, CA: University of Southern California: 1–32.

National Assessment Synthesis Team. 2000. U.S. National Assessment of the Potential Consequences of Climate Variability and Change. U.S. Global Change Research Program. http://www.globalchange.gov/publications/reports/scientific-assessments/first-national-assessment. (January 2010).

National Hispanic Environmental Council, Clean the Air. 2010. Global warming and latinos: a growing threat to our health, economic, and social well-being. 30 p. http://www.nheec.org/LatinoGWFactSheetwithReferences.pdf. (January 10, 2010).

Nilsson, C. 2008. Climate change from an indigenous perspective: key issues and challenges. Indigenous Affairs. 1-2: 9–16.

Ogden, A.; Innes, J. 2009. Application of structured decision making to an assessment of climate change vulnerabilities and adaptation options for sustainable forest management. Ecology and Society. 14(1): 1–24. http://www.ecologyandsociety.org/vol14/iss1/art11/. (August 23, 2009).

Ogunwole, S.U. 2006. We the people: American Indians and Alaska Natives in the United States, census 2000 special reports. Washington, DC: U.S. Census Bureau, U.S. Department of Commerce Economics and Statistics Administration.

Oke, T. 1973. City size and the urban heat island. Atmos. Environ. 7: 769–779.

Orzag, Peter R. 2007. Approaches to reducing carbon dioxide emissions. Testimony before the Committee on the Budget, U.S. House of Representatives. November 1. On file with: Peter Orzag, Congressional Budget Office. Second and D Streets, S.W. Washington, D.C. 20515.

Oxfam America. 2009. Exposed: social vulnerability and climate change in the U.S. Southeast. http://adapt.oxfamamerica.org/resources/Exposed_Report.pdf. (January 15, 2010).

Paavola, J.; Adger, W.N. 2006. Fair adaptation to climate change. Ecological Economics. 56(4): 594–609.

Pandey, N. 2006. Societal adaptation to abrupt climate change and monsoon variability: implications for sustainable livelihoods of rural communities. Jaipur, Rajasthan: Climate and Women Group. On file with: Winrock International India, 1 Navjeevan Vihar, New Delhi 110 017, India. Winrock International India, New Delhi: 211–217.

Parks, B.; Roberts, J.T. 2006. Globalization, vulnerability to climate change, and perceived injustice. Society and Natural Resources. 19(4): 337–355.

Parry, M.L.; Canziani, O.F.; Palutikof, J.P.; van der Linden, P.J.; Hanson, C.E., eds. 2007. Climate change 2007: impacts, adaptation and vulnerability. Contribution of Working Group II to the fourth assessment report of the Intergovernmental Panel on Climate Change. Cambridge, United Kingdom: Cambridge University Press: 1–16.

Puentes, R.; Warren, D. 2006. One-fifth of America: a comprehensive guide to America's first suburbs. Metropolitan Policy Program. Washington, D.C.: The Brookings Institution. 24 p.

Riewe, R.R.; Oakes, J.E., eds. 2006. Climate change: linking traditional and scientific knowledge. Winnipeg, Manitoba: Aboriginal Issues Press. 289 p.

Rosenzweig, C.; Karoly, D.; Vicarelli, M.; Neofotis, P.; Wu, Q.; Casassa, G.; Menzel, A.; Root, T.L.; Estrella, N.; Seguin, B.; Tryjanowski, P.; Liu, C.; Rawlins, S.; Imeson, A. 2008. Attributing physical and biological impacts to anthropogenic climate change. Nature. 453(7193): 353–357.

Schulz, A.J., Williams, D.R.; Israel, B.A.; Lempert, L.B. 2002. Racial and spatial relations as fundamental determinants of health in Detroit. The Milbank Quarterly. Hoboken, NJ: Wiley-Blackwell. 80(4): 677–707.

Shin, L. 2009. Navajo Nation approves first tribal "green jobs" legislation. Solve Climate. July 22. http://solveclimate.com/blog/20090722/navajo-nation-approves-first-tribal-green-jobs-legislation. (July 2009).

Shonkoff, S.B.; Morello-Frosch, R.; Pastor, M. 2009. Environmental health and equity impacts from climate change and mitigation policies in California: a review of the literature. Sacramento, CA: California Climate Change Center. Environmental Justice. 2(4): 173–177.

Smith, K. 2008. Climate change on the Navajo Nation lands. Paper presented at International expert group meeting on indigenous peoples and climate change, Darwin, Australia, April 1, 2008. United Nations University—Institute of Advanced Studies, Secretariat of the United Nations Permanent Forum on Indigenous Issues, North Australian Indigenous Land and Sea Management Alliance. http://www.un.org/esa/socdev/unpfii/documents/EGM_cs08_Smith. doc. (November 2010).

Suagee, D.B. 2009. Suagee: tribal sovereignty and the green energy revolution: the Waxman-Markey Bill. Indian Country Today. July 25. http://www. indiancountrytoday.com/opinion/51570032.html. (July 2009).

Tsosie, R. 2007. Indigenous people and environmental justice: the impact of climate change. University of Colorado Law Review. 78(4): 1625–1678.

United Nations Development Programme [UNDP]. 2000. Building resilience to social vulnerability: a SIDS perspective. http://www.sidsnet.org/docshare/ other/20031104114454_Building_Resilience_to_Social_Vulnerability.ppt. (February 1, 2009).

Wall, E. 2008. Climate change and rural issues: Le plus ca change le plus c'est la même chose. Journal of Rural and Community Development. 3(2): 1–6.

Wall, E.; Marzall, K. 2006. Adaptive capacity for climate change in Canadian rural communities. Local Environment. 11(4): 373–397.

Wesche, S.; Armitage, D. 2006. Adapting to environmental change in a northern delta system. In: Riewe, R.R.; Oakes, J.E., eds. Climate change: linking traditional and scientific knowledge. Winnipeg, Manitoba: Aboriginal Issues Press: 165–184.

Williams, D.R.; Collins, C.A. 2001. Racial residential segregation: a fundamental cause of racial disparities in health. Public Health Reports. 116: 404–416.

Williams, T.; Hardison, P. 2005. Global climate change: environmental change and water law. Paper presented at the law seminars international conference What is Next for Washington Water Law? May 20, 2005. On file with: Preston Hardison, Tulalip Tribes, 6406 Marine Dr., Tulalip, WA 98271.

Williams, T.; Hardison, P. 2007. Global climate change: justice, security and economy. Paper Presented at the Salmon Homecoming Forum. On file with: Preston Hardison, Tulalip Tribes, 6406 Marine Dr., Tulalip, WA 98271.

Williams, T.; Hardison, P. 2008. Global climate change and indigenous peoples. Prepared for the July 31–August 2, Indigenous Treaty Gathering. Lummi, Washington: Tulalip Tribes of Washington. On file with: Preston Hardison, Tulalip Tribes, 6406 Marine Dr., Tulalip, WA 98271.

Wisner, B.; Blaikie, P.; Cannon, T.; Davis, I. 2004. At risk: natural hazards, people's vulnerability, and disasters. London; New York: Routledge. 2nd ed. 134 p.

Appendix: Additional Sources

For all of the literature cited in this synthesis, annotations are available. For a complete list of annotated literature and copies of the annotations, contact: Ellen Donoghue, USDA Forest Service, Pacific Northwest Research Station (edonoghue@ fs.fed.us) and Kathy Lynn, University of Oregon Environmental Studies Program (kathy@uoregon.edu).

Arler, F. 2001. Global partnership, climate change and complex equality. Environmental Values. 10(3): 28.

Bapna, M.; McGray, H.; Mock, G.; Withey, L. 2009. Enabling adaptation: priorities for supporting the rural poor in a changing climate. Washington, DC: World Resources Institute.

Bendixen and Associates. 2008. National survey of Hispanic voters on environmental issues. http://www.sierraclub.org/ecocentro/survey/analysis.pdf. (January 10, 2010).

Boyle, K. 2009. Rivers: Sacramento-San Joaquin tops "most endangered" list. Greenwire. April 7.

Brody, A.; Demetriades, J.; Esplen, E. 2008. Gender and climate change: mapping the linkages—a scoping study on knowledge and gaps. United Kingdom Department for International Development. http://siteresources.worldbank.org/ EXTSOCIALDEVELOPMENT/Resources/DFID_Gender_Climate_Change.pdf. (September 22, 2008).

Burns, D. 2009. Is there an anti-rural bias in climate bill? Daily Yonder. July 17. http://www.dailyyonder.com/there-anti-rural-bias-climate-bill/2009/07/17/2236. (July 22, 2009).

Centre for Indigenous Environmental Resources. 2007. Climate change impacts on abundance and distribution of traditional foods and medicines: effects on a First Nation and their capacity to adapt. Winnipeg: Centre for Indigenous Environmental Resources: 1–35.

Climate Equity Alliance. 2009. Advancing equity through climate solutions: principles for addressing the needs of low and moderate income workers, families, and communities within global warming legislation. http://www. greenforall.org/what-we-do/working-with-washington/climate-equity/. (January 30, 2010).

Corbera, E.; Kosoy, N.; Martınez Tuna, M. 2007. Equity implications of marketing ecosystem services in protected areas and rural communities: case studies from Meso-America. Global Environmental Change. 17: 365–380.

Dankelman, I. 2008. Gender, climate change and human security, lessons from Bangladesh, Ghana and Senegal. Prepared for the Women's Environment and Development Organization. http://www.wedo.org/wp-content/uploads/hsn-study-final-may-20-2008.pdf. (November 15, 2009).

Ebi, K.; Meehl, G. 2007. The heat is on: climate change and heatwaves in the Midwest. Arlington, VA: Pew Center on Global Climate Change: 1–20.

Encheva, M. 2008. The principle of equity in the United Nations framework convention on climate change. Varna, Bulgaria: Technical University: 1–3.

Ermine, W.; Sauchyn, D.; Vetter, M.; Hart, C. 2007. Isi Wipan-climate: identifying the impacts of climate change and capacity for adaptation in two Saskatchewan First Nation communities. Final Research Project to the Prairie Adaptation Research Collaborative. www.parc.ca/pdf/research_publications/isiwipan-final.pdf. (January 2010).

Folke, C. 2006. Resilience: the emergence of a perspective for social-ecological systems analyses. Global Environmental Change. 16: 253–267.

Gable, E. 2009. Damage, pollution from wildfires could surge as Western U.S. warms. Land Letter. http://www.wrapair.org/forums/amc/meetings/091111_Nox/pollution_increases_as_climate_warms_August_6_2009.pdf. (November 2010).

Geman, B. 2009. Climate: Wyden attacks Obama cap-and-trade revenue plan. E&E News PM. Washington, DC: Environment & Energy Publishing. (March 11).

Hartmann, B. 2009. 10 reasons why population control is not the solution to global warming. Different Takes, Climate Change Series No. 57. (Winter 2009). http://popdev.hampshire.edu/sites/popdev/files/uploads/dt/DTakes_57_final.pdf. (January 15, 2010).

Hemmati, M.; Ulrike, R. 2009. Engendering the climate-change negotiations: experiences, challenges, and steps forward. Gender and Development. 17(1): 19–32. http://dx.doi.org/10.1080/13552070802696870. (December 10, 2009).

Hunter, L.M.; David, E. 2009. Climate change and migration: considering the gender dimensions. Working Pap. POP2009-13. Boulder, CO: University of Colorado at Boulder, Institute for Behavioral Science, Population Program. http://www.colorado.edu/IBS/pubs/pop/pop2009-0013.pdf. (November 15, 2009).

International Indian Treaty Council. 2008. Climate change, human rights, and indigenous peoples. Palmer, AK: Submission to the United Nations High Commissioner on Human Rights by the International Indian Treaty Council (IITC), NGO in special consultative status to the UN Economic and Social Council. On file with: Andrea Carmen, Executive Director, IITC Administration Office, 456 N. Alaska St., Palmer, AK 99645.

Leber, J. 2009. Forests: biochar—one way to deal with more fire-prone forests. New York Times. May 1, 2009. http://www.nytimes.com/cwire/2009/05/01/01climatewire-biochar-one-way-to-deal-with-more-fire-prone-12208.html. (May 2009).

MacKendrick, K. 2009. Climate change adaptation planning for cultural and natural resource resilience: a look at planning for climate change in two Native Nations in the Pacific Northwest U.S., Eugene, OR: University of Oregon. M.S. thesis.

Martello, M.L. 2008. Arctic indigenous peoples as representations and representatives of climate change. Social Studies of Science. 38(3): 351–376.

Michaelowa, A.; Michaelowa, K. 2007. Climate or development: Is ODA diverted from its original purpose? Climate Change. 84: 17.

National Assessment Synthesis Team. 2000. Climate change impacts on the United States: the potential consequences of climate variability and change. Washington DC: U.S. Global Change Research Program.

National Latino Coalition on Climate Change. http://latinocoalitionclimatochange.org. (March 11, 2010).

National Wildlife Federation. 2009. The fair climate project: promoting fair and equitable solutions to climate change. http://fairclimateproject.org. (September 5, 2009).

Office of the Chief Economist for the U.S. Department of Agriculture. 2009. A preliminary analysis of the effects of HR 2454 on U.S. Agriculture. http://www.usda.gov/oce/newsroom/archives/releases/2009files/HR2454.pdf. (July 2009).

Oki, T.; Kanae, S. 2006. Global hydrological cycles and world water resources. Science. 313(5790): 1068–1072.

Osterle, A. 2002. Evaluating equity in social policy: a framework for comparative analysis. Evaluation. 8: 46–59.

Oxfam America. 2008. Fact sheet/climate change & women. http://www.wedo.org/wp-content/uploads/ccwomenfactsheet-final.pdf. (January 15, 2010).

Samuelsohn, D.; Bravender, R. 2009. Climate: EPA holds trump card in U.S. emissions debate. Greenwire. April 2.

Suagee, D. 2009. Tribal sovereignty and the green energy revolution: including tribal partners in climate change response. Indian Country Today. September 18. http://www.indiancountrytoday.com/archive/59727607.html. (January 15, 2010).

Turner, N.J.; Clifton, H. 2009. It's so different today: climate change and indigenous lifeways in British Columbia, Canada. Global Environmental Change. 19: 180–190.

United Nations [UN]. 2009. The United Nations framework convention on climate change-Article 3–principles. http://unfccc.int/essential_background/convention/items/2627.php. (February 1, 2009).

U.S. Climate Change Science Program. 2008. Best practice approaches for characterizing, communicating and incorporating scientific uncertainty in climate decision making. Washington, DC.

van Aalst, M.K.; Cannon, T.; Burton, I. 2008. Community level adaptation to climate change: the potential role of participatory community risk assessment. Global Environmental Change. 18(1): 165–179.

Warren, F.J. 2004. Climate change impacts and adaptation: a Canadian perspective. Ottawa, Ontario: Natural Resources Canada. 201 p.

Wood, M.C. 2009. Atmospheric trust litigation. In: Rodgers, W.H., Jr.; Robinson-Dorn, M., eds. Climate Change Reader. Durham, NC: Carolina Academic Press: 1–60.